IN PRA

pointers to

MW00332829

"When you look into the abyss, the abyss also looks into you."
Friedrich Nietzsche

"Pointers to Awakening, An Invitation Into Presence" is a must read for everyone who is on a spiritual journey. I have known Alan Shelton for nearly 25 years, many of the chapters of this incredible manuscript I had the privilege of participating in as a character in his story. There is no logical reason why Alan and I would ever meet, do business together or become close friends, and that as it would seem is exactly the point. Alan from California, Jerry from Kansas, completely different family upbringings and business experiences, yet from the moment Alan and I met we independently knew that we were in the presence of something that was certainly larger than us. We shared the universal language of business, but also shared the collective experience of curiosity, and the joyful responses that get intertwined into diving headfirst into impossibilities.

Oh Man, where there a lot of impossibilities, but each was perfect in their own way, with an outcome attached to them that would serve the collective presence. Alan's teachings created a fearlessness, a deep consciousness of the heart that recognized that there is no threat in new possibilities and in fact you begin to seek out as many of these encounters with presence as humanly possible. This book is a gift to mankind, to those who have decided not to be conformed and defined by the world, but those who are being renewed by their mind to actually see the "Oaktree" in the "Acorn". Alan, brilliant my friend! And much love!

JERRY SKILLETT
Executive Chairman SPACES

Pointers to Awakening is the perfect vehicle to understanding the spiritual journey. Much like the perfect wave that starts simply and then shows its majesty at the crescendo, it is the perfect expression of my time with Alan. I have walked the beaches, jungles and taco joints with Alan. It's always the same. Spirituality is here and now. The tangibility of life cannot be converted to intellectual expression. Such are merely pointers to the simple. We look to masters. Revere them. Glean so much. Trying to find permanence? Safety? Control? The energy is there. The light is there. Only peace in the tangibility is possible as happiness. All externalities crumble. Only from within.

I honestly don't know what would have become of me from not knowing you.

DAN CALLAWAY,
Attorney and Lifelong Friend

I highly recommend *Pointers to Awakening.* As consciousness we are a fascinating combination of the detail in motion of manifestation and the stillness in presence of witnessing. Many parts of Alan's writing trigger satori moments for me. An Inner remembrance or coming home if you will. This is the opening that happens while surfing when the wave and I perfectly merge. And on the wave or in the book my feeling is "of course!"

DONOVAN STAPLETON
Oceanside Surfer, Hill Street Family.

"It is not at all an overstatement to say that Alan's work has utterly transformed the way I understand my life and exactly who and what I am. Even beyond that, his transmission of wisdom through this book gave me the ability to act in accordance with this understanding in every area of my life RIGHT NOW. "

JAYA DANIEL
Executive and Seeker

Pointers to Awakening is the deep dive into story and the magic of consciousness that sustains it. Finding your own original myth is one of Alan's devices that I did with my wife, Marise. Our stories came through like a bolt of lightning as we discovered while we shared ours. There we sat in awe and laughter. Living and loving our story while adventuring into the authenticity of the spiritual journey. *Pointers to Awakening* is a must for the serous spiritual seeker!

JAMES BEAUFAIT
Retired IBM Executive

Alan Shelton's *Pointers to Awakening* is, like Alan himself, a sweet surprise that sometimes isn't immediately obvious.

I "eat" books that are rife with truth like potato chips. It is difficult to get enough because each one makes more hugely anticipated. I also go into a new book thinking, "I already know all of this, but reminders are very useful." Literally, little did I know.

Alan is a storyteller. His stories are not randomly thrown in — every one of them is a fable worth devouring. And I do know there is always more for me to learn. He delivers. Not the least of it is the author's distinction between knowledge seeking and wisdom seeking. In my own words, the knowledge path is one of "storing truths" and the wisdom path is "knowing in the moment". Alan's gift is wisdom. Wisdom comes not as knowing or beliefs; it comes whole, in our heart.

At one point he states this: "There is only one thing to know. We live in a state of misidentification. Every, and I mean every, pointer is dedicated to dissolving, obliterating and shattering that false story. That's it."

Paradoxically, and gratefully, there is that only thing to know, but it is the only thing to know so we can allow the light to come in when it is present. This book is a rich resource for the wisdom call, a.k.a. pointers.

MILES KIERSON
Retired Leadership Guru

Pointers to Awakening is a timeless gift of the ages. It is a must read particularly now when the Western world is seeking the deeper answers to life's purpose and existence itself.

As a lifelong Spiritual Seeker, it was immediately obvious upon meeting Alan that he exuded presence. Little did I know this presence would weave together my lifetime of seeking with all its associated gaps and nest them within his Ageless Wisdom.

Alan is rooted in an Exalted lineage of Spiritual Masters/ Sages dating back to Ramana Maharshi to Nisargadatta Maharaj to Ramesh Balsekar. And now it's Alan who is referred to as a modern-day Master/Sage.

It was Ramesh Balsekar who suggested Alan bring this Ageless wisdom to the Western mind, a task many have tried with little success. Wow, did he ever. Alan has a unique and brilliant way of taking the seemingly complex Spiritual Terrain and delivering its Divine purity with such subtlety and simplicity.

Within this simplicity one truly experiences the absolute possibility of consciousness and knowing that this Exalted state is who they really are.

It is easy for me to make things sound wonderful, but there is simply no space for embellishment here. This work deserves the highest praise. It is an instant spiritual classic with nothing like it in modern print. Chapter 23…just WOW! What a service to the spiritual seeker. My goodness, the clarity of the delivery of that chapter is a game changer.

RON ARIO
Real Estate Entrepreneur and Friend

Alan's style of working and writing is very available and ordinary and that's why he's so special. Awakening has been made special by the spiritually misguided and is anything but. Pointers to Awakening is direct, simple and compelling. Alan has often been called the "food truck" style of spiritual chef. That he is.

TOIVO HALVORSEN
JD, MBA and current student of Alan

Pointers to Awakening is a modern masterpiece. It is perfect for our Westernized got-to-know-everything mindset. It is the missing puzzle piece for helping us to understand, and be ok with, this mysterious journey called life. I cannot express my gratitude anywhere near enough. If you're a genuine seeker, this is for you. My entire life revolves around the most unbelievable coincidences which is exactly how I came to unexpectedly meet Alan Shelton during an online event. Like all enlightened masters Alan's wisdom and insights are priceless and I consider myself very fortunate and blessed indeed to be his friend.

NAMASTE,
JULIAN ROBUS, THE HICK THAT WOKE UP
Happy Onion Living

Not only have I read Alan's words, but I was in the inaugural Spiritual MBA group based on *Pointers to Awakening.* I wish I could convey the magnitude and gratitude of the impact of this experience but alas these words would not only do it no justice, but I expect that they would be met with a smattering of disbelief. Much better for me to offer a humble request to read *Pointers to Awakening.* And if you find yourself in procession of a very special invitation to join a Satsang group or Spiritual MBA with dear brother Alan, take a leap of faith into the unknown. You will realize that you are in possession of the most glorious of gifts, a golden ticket to a life more fulfilled, more vivid, and colorful and certainly more enriched! For every minute you spend in his presence is akin to drinking from the never-ending wisdom fountain of knowing - tears, joy and belly laughs will ensue. Be sure to play all out and embrace your inner child - this wisdom wrapped in a book is your gateway and invitation - know that it's not in your hands by accident.

KRISTIAN KEMERY-TOONE
Entrepreneur, Special Projects Consultant

POINTERS TO
awakening

also by Alan E. shelton

awakened Leadership
Beyond self-mastery

Pointers to Awakening

An invitation into presence

by

Alan E. Shelton

Red Hatchet Press | 2021

ISBN 978-0-9847125-3-3
SOFTCOVER

ISBN 978-0-9847125-6-4
EBOOK

BOOK & COVER DESIGN
JOHN BALKWILL, LUMINO PRESS

COVER PHOTOS
RENEE FOX

Dedication

This book is dedicated to all of my Grandchildren, and you are invited to be one.

From Grandpa Ed to Ramesh, I have been cherished as a grandchild and the mantle of 'Abuelo' has now been given to me. It is in this loving and sacred essence that a Grandfather can point to the natural place where we all are one. To the natural place where we are all awakened.

To Sonny, Lincoln, Lashai, Tray-Sean, Yasmine, Paolo, Amire and my grandchildren to come, I am eternally grateful. You have allowed this old man to love you, teach you, and hold you on my lap. We share presence and now…we freely give that to all who want to come home.

contents

part one

Pointers To Awakening

part two

The Magic of Story

part Three

Looking Under the Hood

part four

Facing Life

Epilogue

AUTHOR'S PREFACE

Do you sense that there is something missing in your life? Do you feel a lack of harmony? Are you disillusioned, or in distress, or even misery? Have you taken one too many rides at the Disneyland for the Spiritual and wonder when you will finally wake up? Is your life delivering what you want or truly need? Yep, I've been there. In fact, I left a burgeoning career from corporate America as a merger acquisition certified public accountant at the age of thirty-seven in 1990 and travelled to India to seek. Seek what? I honestly didn't know. I just knew that there was something deeply wrong and I wanted to find someone, anyone, who really knew and felt and even embodied some answers.

So, in early 1990, I made my first trip to India. I had recently heard an Indian mystic named Osho speak. The banal and the sublime bumped shoulders on this one. I had a business appointment to meet the owners of several large commercial properties. I arrived at their office and noticed some books on the table with this Indian man named Osho featured on the cover. It turns out one of the owners had been with Osho for years and the corporate building I was in doubled as a meditation center! After ten minutes of business talk, I was led into the meditation hall where I heard Osho speak for the first time. When he described the ego, I instantly got it. He knew what he was talking about.

He said the ego was a tangible movement, not even an entity or personality, attempting to carve its own way to be in charge despite the wave of consciousness inviting all into its keep. Meaning ego was an energy force but it didn't have a chance because of the vastness of consciousness. This was the first frame I had of my seeking search. The ego was a disrupter. It didn't have a chance, if and only if, we could get it to butt out. Otherwise, it would persist looking to all the world like it belonged, even though knowing it didn't. Now it was on! This truly struck me like a bolt of lightning. I can't say it enough. I knew he knew. And like any starving man, I headed to the food supply! That impression was so profound and so strong that I was compelled to instantly change my life!

After only a few weeks from the time I heard Osho speak, I was on a plane to India, where I spent the majority of the next 7 years! I sold my large business after my first three months' visit, as well as my home! But it was important that I keep a set of clients that I still served. Osho exhorted his seekers to return to the marketplace. It was in the marketplace that the pointers for awakening that he taught could really operate. What would it be worth if a spiritual awakening lived only in a remote cave in India? Osho felt the cave dwelling mystics were fooling themselves. Awakening lives in the marketplace and in the culture-- that is the gift and contribution from the blossoming within. And so, I began to study and practice and eventually repurpose spiritual concepts into corporate leadership language. Why? I lived in a world I could actually penetrate to share some of the teachings of the mysteries of life itself from the teachers and mystics I embraced. This was only the beginning of my seeking.

I met my next teacher in 1997. His name was Prasad, and he was the first of the non-dualists. What's a non-dualist? If the ego depends on separation to exist, it must live in duality. What's the human response? To see from a place of non-separation or non-duality. But the ego conundrum has a doorway out! A friend of my wife, Justine, and also an Osho sannyasin casually mentioned that some fellow was holding a Satsang in Encinitas, California. I wandered in with my typical skeptical sense and listened to Prasad locate story. Where was it? It lived in duality and was simply a rendering. My Osho life, which was a wide and unconnected body of understandings began to materialize in a way I never yet knew. Yes, Osho was himself a non-dualist, but he was a hundred other things as well. The Osho experience coalesced in understanding the value and power of story and this was the next step. I was thrust into my finishing, as it were, but this beginning needed an ending.

In 1998 I had the opportunity to read the writings of a mystic and teacher named Ramesh Balsekar. It was upon reading Ramesh for the first time that my own journey began to make sense, at least as much as a spiritual journey can make sense. It was a coalescing of internal-ness, felt, but not intellectualized. Why? Well, it happened on its own. The doorbell of Presence then rang when I had what I call my awakening experience, in 1999. I guess it's appropriate for a 5th generation Californian to experience such a thunderbolt on the 405-freeway headed north to Century City. Yep, how appropriate! In a moment, my entire world shifted from the perspective of ego to that of pure awareness itself.

How to describe awakening to you? Most avoid this as the actual describing reduces the ineffable into the mundane. But to be clear…It all begins with a living understanding that there is such a possibility built into our very essence. Often, seekers have momentary experiences that last from minutes to weeks which I like to call free samples. It all boils down to something very simple. As an ego we feel we are separate from all else to such a degree that we believe we are autonomous authors of our own journey. Our experience is that we, as a body and mind, are doing something that we are controlling. Awakening is simply the emergence of our original state which is one of being lived through by Presence itself rather than something separate living it. This sounds intellectual but it's not. The feelings of relief and peace are palpable as one can look out and recognize that you and all else are the same thing in the flow of things. You are simply relaxed into that movement. The felt experience of this is felt to the bottom of all that is. By whom? By consciousness itself, as the rendered story of you as the ego is seen yet simply bypassed. And so there I am on the freeway, the 'free-way?', and my felt bondage shed instantaneously. I experienced the perfect harmonization with the flow of life. I no longer was forcing myself into ego identification and its bondage and control. The sense of being a seeker driven to unearth at all costs also evaporated. Perceiving was happening but not identified with the character called Alan. The sense of permanent peace filled the space that the ego used to occupy. Ahhh.

I physically met my next teacher, Ramesh, after that experience. Ramesh was much more of a mentor than the rest of my spiritual teachers who were forming a lineage of sorts. He truly spoke into my own trajectory as my seeking dynamic had dropped away. I was now simply a possibility that Ramesh could coach and mentor through the integration, bumpy as it is, as this awakening event established itself within Alan's activities. I so appreciated the Satsang, a seeker's gathering, that he offered every morning. For twenty-four years, Ramesh had offered this seeker's gathering every day. Only in India would a makeshift gang of spiritual aspirants line up across the street to be guided up the four floors to the flat where the meeting took place. All attendees were instructed to arrive 30 minutes prior to the Satsang and locate across the street from the house of Ramesh. That half hour before the two-hour Satsang would include what the streets of India always provide--A mashup of animals, beggars, sadhus, and rickshaws along with every scent existing on earth, weaving an experience that screamed Mumbai! This was the perfect preface for a spiritual gathering. From the marketplace of crushing humanity to the sacred sitting with a master.

By the time I arrived at Ramesh's door in 2005, my seekers' drive had long left my body-mind in the awakening event as I described. This particular trip to India was one of love and celebration. As luck would have it, on most days Ramesh had the time to play mentor with me. We'd meet in the afternoon for our conversations and a cup of tea. Ramesh had been a graduate of the London School of Economics and the CEO for the Bank of India, and since I had a corporate history as a merger/acquisition expert and later a CEO for several companies we shared the same language and similar views of the world inside and out. This common attribute of framing concepts gave our afternoon chats the feeling of two men sharing a life's journey.

Ramesh took this opportunity to encourage me to write and publish the story of my own spiritual journey. He explained that the western world was hungry for the tangibility of such a story. Folks had come for many years from western countries to commune with the masters and sages of India. But, in effect, they had become accustomed to leaning on and borrowing the tangible spiritual framework available in the East. His view was that the time had come for the West, and particularly America, to begin to tell its own awakening stories in its own voice, inclusive of the customs and context that exist there. In his view he saw that I should enter this fray by writing my own story. Ramesh would tell me that awakening must naturally appear in whatever cultural construct it occupies. "The West has been borrowing from the East for many years and long enough. Go create your version." I often look back and see that this particular visit shaped what has become the rest of my life.

Ramesh laid out his view of the transmission of awakening wisdom. It was, as he called it, a living understanding. Each carrier of the awakened story of consciousness delivered that story in a way that only he or she could. Yes, there was only one consciousness and that is what every one of us is. But much like snow is the only ingredient of a snowflake, each one is uniquely its own form, notwithstanding the singularity of its very essence of content. Resultantly, I would begin to express a series of teachings that would be unique and could be called "my teachings". This was true even though as a speaker of consciousness I was only a conduit for the pass through of concepts or stories, as I would take to calling such bits.

I did exactly that in a book entitled *Awakened Leadership*, which had my twist of corporate and spiritual language. It was what one might expect from a kid raised in California in the sixties whose life had included equal parts of corporate acumen and spiritual searching. What qualifies someone like me to even attempt such a crazy combination? Simple. My experience is the product of two major movements. The spiritual search and the corporate or market construct. At the intersection of these two, it can be easily seen that what looks like two different things are actually the same. Leadership development is the same path as spiritual awakening in many ways. Yes, the corporate path stops short, since the ego achievement is seen as the goal. But many of us arrive at that point knowing that there is something more. Our intuition broadcasts that this is the case and creates an extended internal misery for many of us. And so, some of us become seekers. And sometimes teachers. And sometimes both. And often a lineage is born.

Those who have inspired my path may scoff at the notion of a lineage. But many of us who have experienced an awakening speak from that place. That includes my teachers Ramana Maharshi, Nisargadatta Maharaj, Osho, Papaji, Ramesh Balsekar, Robert Adams and Prasad. But wait! What about all of the mentors and influencers in my life that went before the list of the spiritual versions. They, too, were immensely influential in my life. My grandfather, a CPA and founder of a Pontiac dealership in San Diego, sat me in his lap whilst telling me stories of the great philosophers, among others. My business career included mentors such as Milton Friedman, Peter Drucker and Stephen Covey. Yep, each of these took me personally under his wing to season and develop, as they saw it, my potential. This may not amount to a lineage but belonging to a channel of movement seemingly amounts to the same.

Although corporate and spiritual messaging might not appear synchronous, it is in many ways. We all use pointers in wisdom to help seekers along. But the common denominator with corporate leaders and spiritual mystics is something I coin as presence. Always presence. The felt experience of leadership was, and can be, the felt experience of enlightenment, a magnetizing presence. My corporate mentors would tell me that one knows a great leader the minute you are around them. Same as one knows a great mystic.

One of my favorite TV shows some years back was called *The West Wing*. There is a scene that has always seemed to fit the state of deep inauthenticity that my life seemed to follow. I renamed it as the story "The Seeker's Hole".

A guy walking down the street falls into a hole. The sides are so steep that it seems impossible to get out, but he tries anyway. He keeps at it, hour after hour, slipping back down again on each attempt.

After a while, he realizes that he can see who's walking by if he cranes his neck at the correct angle. A doctor passes by, and the guy shouts up, "Hey, you . . . can you help me out?" The doctor writes a prescription, throws it down the hole, and moves on. Not long afterward, a priest comes along, and the guy yells out, "Father, I'm down in this hole; please, can you help me?" The priest scribbles down a prayer, throws it down the hole, and moves on. Then, to the man's elation, one of his friends walks by. "Joe, it's me! Am I ever glad to see you! Give me some help here, okay?"

At this, the friend jumps into the hole, and our guy says, "Are you stupid? Now we are both down here!"

His friend says, "Yeah, but I've been down here before and I know how to get out."

It turns out that I was always looking for my guy. The one who had been in the hole before and knew the way out. And I found him. He appeared in a number of forms along the way, but I found him. And I am forever grateful.

It took me some time to realize that my natural inclination to teach with story should feed and inspire my next writing. *Pointers To Awakening* was born from the desire to do just that. It's filled with story. When you hear me tell a Buddha story, I am likely borrowing from Osho. When you hear me unreel a philosopher's story you can be sure my grandpa was involved. When you hear me talk of Mumbai and India, often Ramesh is in the mix. The business stories are all extracted from my personal experience and that is where Stephen Covey and Peter Drucker will be heard. In this book I have used those stories often and you will hear them as you go along. You will notice that none of these are cited in any way. All of them are from my own experience and I am simply conveying my version in the tradition of oral storytelling and retelling. You cannot deny story is the most innate form of intellectual emergence for humanity itself. It is the first cognizable output of being, crossing the gulf from non-duality to the dual world most hold as real. It must follow that story lives closest to the dense and wet pool of awakening.

So, what makes this book something that you might want to read? It's pretty simple. The spiritual search is incredibly simple in that it is single faceted. Leaning into presence is the entirety of the exercise. That's the good news. The bad news is that our intellectual concept of life, the one that organizes our reality, is simply wrong. And if it were only a replacement of that concept, we could elab-orate the correct one and everyone could move along com-pletely nourished. But it's just not that easy. We live our life "as if" our flimsy belief systems are correct. Those become our assumptive behavior. And after large portions of "as if" over a lifetime, that behavior informs our concepts, and our concepts inform our behavior.

Yep, you got it. We live in a feedback loop, the same one

as everyone else. And like the emperor with no clothes, we eagerly proclaim to all that indeed there are clothes, and nice ones at that! Remember the movie Groundhog Day? The internal notification that drives most of us to seek spiritually is simply the intuitive recognition that we are in a loop that seemingly cannot be exited. But it can. We have to go back and find the place where we took the wrong exit and get back on the freeway of consciousness. We can't avoid the knowledge that we are inauthentic renderings of what someone else felt we should be.

You likely feel it is no longer possible to ignore the discomfort of your own inauthenticity. Is that your fault? Nope. You inherited it from likely well-meaning folks that were equally self-deceived. Leaving the world of the misidentification of yourself, the one that intuitively self-communicates that there is something deeply wrong, is like a space capsule leaving the gravity of the earth. The reminder to keep going and not forget the direction of movement is critical to both seekers and space capsules as it turns out. This book is intended to play those roles. Just for you, not for space capsules!

As my own misconceptions vanished in my spiritual awakening, I was prodded beyond simply writing to create a platform on which those from my world could understand the spiritual journey. Being a corporate kind of a guy, I helped create a web presence called Globalish to deliver an awakening point of view to stories of the day to the corporate minded seekers. I spent my days answering questions supplied to me by my partner, Michael Richardson, and others. Additionally, a small cadre of seekers of all kinds began to show up in our offices in Los Angeles. This led to a turnstile version of incoming and outbound seekers engaged in a Satsang conversation with me. There were no beginning or ending hours. Just show up and drop into the ongoing conversation.

After some months of this activity, those around me began to notice that I used certain concepts and stories to attempt to deconstruct the assumed notions that made up our life as we claimed they happened. Michael, in his understated brilliance, decided to create a Facebook page in which folks could post the concepts I was using. It was in this moment that I realized that my beloved Ramesh was right. I had been delivering a set of my own pointers even though I could never claim them as mine. He was correct. I had my own teachings.

But why do this? To reiterate, it turns out that the conditioning in the East holds that when it comes to the spiritual, one simply enters and exits any spontaneous conversation as a part of the cultural behavior. Westerners, however, want to know the map, or the terrain as I call it. Yes, I refashioned many of the awakening concepts I understood into corporate and Western terminology. I answered multitudes of questions and, as the corporate mind is wont to do, the responses began to create a terrain. I could see how to communicate from a series of unrelated responses, a sense of solidity that one could feel under their feet.

What can I pass on now that I couldn't way back in those early days? I know what the spiritual journey is and what it is not. And it is so easy to be deceived. We live in an age where anything remotely non-rational is delegated to the category of the spiritual. Fairies, ascended masters, space aliens, and woo-hoo smoothies all compete for the annual title of dolphin sprinkle spirituality. If what you seek is the Rose Parade version of consciousness, that is not what you will find here. The spiritual journey is real, robust, and tangible and it requires an unending supply of tenacity or earnestness. This rocket propelled spiritual search is often said to be looking for awakening. Other times it is called enlightenment or authenticity. I now call it Presence. These are all the same thing. And it is real. It happens. It is the epitome of authenticity. The rise of Presence is consciousness, introducing itself.

Awakening to your natural authentic self is a possibility. The presence that you are will rise as a result. It takes a single focus, intense dedication, and stories and teachings. In my Spiritual Disneyland there would be only one ride. It would be called the "Who Am I Really?" ride. What you hold in your hands is simply one version of the map for that ride. Why read this one? Well, I have been there, and I know the way through.

"Mind is interested in what happens, while awareness is interested in the mind itself. The child is after the toy, but the mother watches the child, not the toy."

NISARGADATTA MAHARAJ

introduction

—•◦ ⚙ ◦•—

THE SEEKER'S JOURNEY

B AM. THE FIRST MOMENT. I don't remember how old I was, maybe around two. I suspect I was in my crib. But I do remember the experience, and there were two things I can render into language. One, I knew I existed. "I am." The second was that I knew there was an "out there" separate from an "in here." In my case, it was seeing the corner of my room where the white ceiling and two-colored walls met. A seemingly banal visual, for certain. But a profound insight. "I am separate from that." Duality was born. "Out there" is a strong process of cognition itself. You might notice that in order for me to convey that first moment, or any moment for that matter, I have constructed a story. It's a very simple story, but it is still a story.

That's what we naturally do.

It's like the intellectual exhaust that tells the man on the street a vehicle has recently passed. We don't get to experience the vehicle itself, but we get the constructed linguistic output, with its particular fumes, commonly called a story. We then take that story and attempt to animate it within our own intellect to understand or onboard the event itself.

In essence, we attempt to recreate experience relying on our own past-recorded tangibility to fill in the fact that we aren't in the moment of experience at all. We are simply in a map or geography called a story. This process is so important that I assert that story is the foundational basis of life, as we know it, and certainly of the seeker's journey. It's not the basis of experience itself, because unpackaged, raw experience is unintelligible. Cognition is the process of packaging, which is constantly reinventing and reinforcing itself. Story is the first and consistent output of all cognition from the moment that we have recorded history, from the moment we "see a corner in a room." How do we know that? All recorded history as we know it is rendered in story, just as we render it today.

One of the first things to notice when entering into a process around your own awakening is that you likely are already laden with assumptions that have become an unseen basis of how you actually think and render stories for yourself. In my first little story I point out that there were two first primal experiences. One was that of the felt experience of existence, while the other was the inference that there is something "out there", as it were. These two elements also are the very definition of duality, a term you will now begin to hear way too much. But duality is so ingrained in how we believe things happen that we can't see another possibility. There is me "in here" and stuff "out there".

Now, awakening is equated with non-duality or a perception, often called apperception, in which the two obvious elements of first cognition no longer arise as separate noticing's. There is the gap we need to cross, and the only way is through what I call pointers. In my teachings these are largely story pointers. The intellect cannot cross this gap. Its existence relies entirely on a construction extracted from the event. Your intuition, the inner knowing of consciousness itself, is the bridge back. That's the good news. The not so good news is that our intuition has been in the back seat for so long it's as irretrievable as your first iPhone.

Since that moment of first cognition, it is likely that you, like most all of us, have been taught to look over and over again to the "out there" part of your experience. In fact, you have built quite a library of stuff that is assumed to inhabit that place. That assumption, which then births others like it, is fully promulgated and supported by those you are supposed to trust the most. These "out there" assumptions crawl into the dark corners to bend how you believe "it is". These assumptions are the coats of old paint, lying under the latest version of what you show others, which unerringly deliver you to the same old dead end on the awakening road. Story utilized in pointer fashion can place you closer to the "here and now" than the stale narrative that crusts the mechanics of your cognitive equipment. So be prepared to challenge much of what you hold near and dear.

In simple terms, seekers need to know that a sense of awkwardness and discomfort is likely to become the co-pilot on the awakening journey. Why? It is because a new revealing is seeking to replace the old conditioning. Until there arises a new listening and cognitive map, this discomfort will pervade. But do not mistake this lack of comfortability in the awakening discussion as signifying a marker in the journey. All of this is just a concept and awakening is anything but.

MOVE THE EGO TO THE CO-PILOT SEAT

The nature of story and how we are conditioned to believe we are a story is largely a mystery. Consciousness moves through each of us as a conduit and we take certain actions. We then take delivery of those actions not on behalf of consciousness but on behalf of our ego self. In other words, we are taught to insert this ego entity by all of our society. This ego self is also called our story identity. In this way we egoically are a living understanding. The story of you, as an ego, is living itself into being.

But what if we were to perceive that the ego "only" was simply not the case? We would see that consciousness lives us directly and there is no extra story that has any reality. We would then begin to onboard another living understanding once we saw this mistaken version of identity. The development of this kind of understanding involves both the intellect and consciousness itself, usually in the form of intuition. It is clear that intellect cannot reach into the pre-verbal world. But that is where our unconscious behaviors seem to live. There is an interchange between the intellect and consciousness itself. But we really don't know how that happens. The idea is to create a new living understanding. Once this takes root and becomes a permanent feature of day-to-day life it is often referred to as awakening or enlightenment. It is marked by the abiding sense of permanent peace which the egoic state never delivers.

Ultimately, for the seeker to emerge from his hole he needs to see that his intellect does not run his world. It is not the pilot in authoring outcomes. Is it a good navigator? Why yes, it is. And that is exactly where we want it to function. Moving the ego, an intellectual construction, from the pilot's seat to the co-pilot's seat is another way to explain this whole process.

THE INTELLECTUAL MAP
CANNOT HOLD AWAKENING

Like all those who write and speak about seeking and awakening, I labor under the restrictions of language itself. The nature of written construction is exactly in the same category of all intellectual processes, that is to say it is an exercise in separation. There is this and there is that. If it is not this then might it be something else? Each word breaks up a flow that may be simply wordless. For this reason, I often point to the distinction between tangibility in being and its representational map. The latter holds all that intellect can produce. Which obviously is far less than everything!

Said map either pretends or is consistently conflated with the very tangibility which births it. Much like birth, the process only works one way, from the womb outwards. Believing birth can be reversed is much like believing the map itself is emergent in any way. The map is constructed and dead in its processed form. But a tangible experience is the territory, and its story is part of the map. One is primary and the other a symbol, no matter how elegantly constructed.

The conditioning of the egoic individual in humanity as we know it today is to live in the map of intellectuality and claim it as being. Since it is the only way we know and it lives unquestioned, the intellectual map is seen as holding something of essence, which it never can. Awakening is the original perception of arising experience. Dualism is the belief that separation is the only state of being, rather than seeing it is simply a conditioned way of seeing.

And what is the result of a life lived in the separation of dualism embracing fully the identified ego? One of my favorite quotes of all time is that of Shakespeare in the play Macbeth. What is life lived in the ego-drama?

"Out, out, brief candle!
Life's but a walking shadow, a poor player
That struts and frets his hour upon the stage
And then is heard no more. It is a tale
Told by an idiot, full of sound and fury,
Signifying nothing."

From Your Story
into the Awakened Story

Imagine for a moment that you carry a story, let's call it your first story. It is populated with seemingly autonomous individuals, often called egos, that author through their own seemingly free will the course that you identify with. You are but one of these supposed egos. But then it happens that an instinct or intuition arises in you that pushes you to find a new story. Usually there is a gnawing sense that something is amiss. This sense pervades all that you do. You begin to look at the world outside and notice the stories generated in every generation that question whether what you see makes sense. In fact, you actually feel in bondage to this story and want to feel free. So off you go to engage in experience that will allow you to reconstruct a story that makes you feel free. If you recognize this story you are a proud member of the seekers club, for you are a seeker. That's great news.

But here is the not-so-great news that goes with it. Most seekers never find the place that feels free. Why? Seekers habitually reconstruct their stories with autonomous individuals, called egos, who through their own free will author their own course in what we call life. Remember, you can't get there from here. What to do? Or what to not do?

Now imagine a world in which all that appears, including you, is actually a whole arising. There are no egos that self-author anything but there is a single operating element that is described as consciousness. That consciousness is actually who you are. Now that is a different story! As it turns out, it's the awakened story. Both of these imaginings are concepts that have been constructed by intellect and rendered into a map called story. It's the experience of the second, the awakened story, that allows the story to be told. The mystic or sage or teachers' charge is to tell a story that pushes the seeker into the awakened story. Many times, this is referred to as a living understanding. Why? It is attempting to replace the story that has you in bondage and hoping it's thrust will be migrated into living itself.

You Can Awaken from Anywhere

Awakening is nothing more but the recognition by consciousness of its own self as a single-arising inclusive of manifestation. That said, manifestation itself encompasses not only the single dream of awakening but also a multiplicity of egoic dreams that live in separation. These separate expressions of ego, in a tangible and lived form, squabble among themselves for superiority - for this is the nature of separation itself. However, all of these supposed separate versions of consciousness are included in the single arising of consciousness itself.

Applied awakening is the simple pointing from the separate to the whole. And why is this important? Because everybody's mind is assumed to be separate, and even the author of its own journey, within this separation. All of us likely assume we are separate and live in an equally distinct terrain of one kind or another. We may be spiritual seekers, entrepreneurs, musicians, or simply commentators upon life as we see it. And through our constant travel in a specific terrain, we become facile with the particulars of that tangible experience. It is by utilizing those particulars from those specific terrains that we can point to the deeper foundational experience of who we really are as a single consciousness. From that pointing, the movement towards awakening begins.

Unlike many traditions that have gone before which specifically assigned awakening to a spiritual category and none of the others, we acknowledge the white space of utilizing the territory upon which we stand as the warehouse of possible pointers to move us into the awakened space of right perception. Start where you are.

It's All Story or Is It?

Life as delivered outside any present moment can only be rendered in a story. Story is a material of which the human map is made. Original myth stories, archetypal stories, fairy tales and gossip all have their position in this platform. Story is the most innate form of intellectual emergence for humanity itself. It is the first cognizable output of being, crossing the gulf from non-duality to the dual world most hold as real. It must follow that story lives closest to the wet pool of awakening and that the kick of a *pointer* could deliver the awakening outcome. This is a dive into the depths of how story lives within our consciousness and why it carries such power.

But the first important possibility in the descent into the basement of stories is to see that you, in your very essence, may not be the story you always have assumed that you are. Secondly, it might be revealed that you are not a story of any kind. And were either of these revelations an underpinning of your everyday movement; would that shift internally the unconscious way in which you experience every moment? That inquiry, and only that inquiry, matters in the long run. The utilization of story is simply my concept, or better said a concept utilizing the Alan intellect as a conduit.

So, notice that the very basis of the question "life is story" actually isn't the case. Life arises and is experienced. It's then packaged as a story by our intellectual equipment. They are not the same thing. But story is as close as we can get, as once the event is in the past so is the experience of it. This may seem like a niggling difference but it's not. We will come back to the difference between what arises to be experienced and its story time and time again.

It turns out that about 70% of all learning in our Western culture is actually accomplished through story. However, in our long-held worship and adoration of the scientific approach, we long ago assigned story and myth to a lower rung of intellectual achievement than our grand theories, statistics, formulas, and their accompanying models. As a result, we have unwittingly narrowed our sense of creativity and discovery by insisting that all questions have literal and highly defined empirical answers. By doing so, we have foregone the joy of a world with creative depth and abandonment in favor of quantifiable so-called answers. And without noticing, that bias has become more embedded in a digital platform that loves nothing more than the choice between zero and one.

Mistaken Identity

There is only one pursuit in the seekers journey—to awaken and have presence emerge as it has to be in awakening. Again, that requires the recognition, through perception, of your proper identity. That's right. The entire world you assume around you is more than likely a case of mistaken identity. The supposed ego is simply an identification that we all seem to make with the separate body-mind that we believe we inhabit. In simple words, our mind and consciousness identify with something separate. That something is roughly defined by your body and mind.

The body/mind is equipped to distinguish one thing from another. That activity of separation is extended into the assumption that each body/mind roughly is tightly bound as an autonomous decision-making entity. The ego is born. This mistaken identity is assumed in every life possibility, delivering a life "as if" separation were true and that each of these entities has a beginning and end. All of our stories are then inhabited by these separate entities. But is this true? This is essentially the seekers search.

It is inevitable that we arrive at this fake identity, as it were. As children we are modeled and taught this identity. We may even have the awareness to wonder if what we were being gifted, so to speak, was remotely close to the case. But the avalanche of learning aimed at us as children is more than a small one could resist. Society had us 'drink from a firehose,' as the saying goes. We've spent our childhood overwhelmed or inundated with an uncapped, unfiltered amount of mistaken identity clues and cues.

But did our teachers, parents, role models themselves, know the identity that they were promoting? Nope. As you know, science in all of its disciplines, is constantly discovering the new version of who we are. And in the meantime, we all unconsciously agree to assume that what we have created as our story thus far will be pressed into daily service "as if" it were the case. Humankind at large lives the quintessential definition of the unexamined life. Or more precisely the unexamined story. And so, do we.

This book, and the entire seeker's journey, is an inquiry into that unexamined, assumed story. Who am I? No really, who am I? This path of self-examination has been trod by mystics and masters for thousands of years. In each cultural context, the search for one's Self is reconstituted and re-emerges. Awakening is a phenomenal possibility and reality. But, as humans, we believe that we are separate and autonomous. We identify with our own particular story version of ourselves, and that identification obscures the presence that we truly are.

Presence

About now you must be thinking "Why does this man blather on so about presence?" I do so because it is key to our movement out of the seeker's misery. All that misery amounts to is simply the noticing, and internal response to, the incongruity we trod every day. Most folks never notice and form the walking dead, initiating all who pass by with the same so-called life formation they have embraced.

That's the story. But stop for a moment and consider. Do you know that you exist? Can you locate the sense that tells you that you are? Is there a sense in every moment that the same you is here that was here when you were five years old? No aging, no attributes, just being here. What does that amount to? A sense of existence that perceives exactly the same no matter what other identification metrics you add on.

What is presence? You might say it is the stable witness behind the ego that blossoms into consciousness. What is the stable witness? That sameness. I am here and I am immutably the same! This is the wisdom path. Presence anchors the journey. But it isn't a set of definitions. It is a sense not a sentence.

The Truth?

We have been taught for a lifetime that there is something called truth. In fact, we will argue incessantly with friends, relatives and strangers about issues with the belief that winning an argument pushes us closer to the truth. We are in the mode of attack. On the spiritual path this lifetime assumption is simply thrown overboard. All we know is that we exist. The rest is simply interpretation and often mixed with judgement.

But wait, isn't there something more than that? What indeed is truth? Who knows? But the dropping of the notion and ingrained behavior that happens unconsciously is the time worn first step of seeking. That is simply to say that we unconsciously fight for what we believe is truth as though our life depended on it. In fact, many claim that our truth claims nest in our drive for survival. But untangle truth from survival and you will see that not only does it not depend on it, but the unconscious activity of attack must be rooted out in order to see what lies beyond. How can that happen? Our notion of truth must be abandoned and replaced with a new approach. All you will find within this writing is that new approach. It's called a pointer.

STORY AND POINTERS

My life's work is an exposition to a set of pointers that utilize story as their basis. How did that happen? As I mentioned in the preface, a friend of mine, Michael Richardson Borne, and I formed a company years back called Globalish. On the surface, we intended to test how a message of non-separation would portray itself in the world of internet engagement. However, in order to support our initiative, I was turned loose in the corporate leadership and development world. That allowed me to begin to test what I called pointers.

I am sure that few except Michael knew that our work was an experiment utilizing the corporate world as a laboratory for likely something bigger than most could dream. But that was how story utilized as a platform for pointers for awakening began to emerge. It all started innocently enough. I had already been active in taking contracts with many of the large brand companies to work with their senior executives. In fact, I had written a book that saw all platforms of life experience as a place for awakening. For awakening only happens in the present moment, and if your moments are spent in the corporate world then that becomes the only place the present moment exists. My job was to teach senior executives how to be authentic such that they would exude presence and wisdom. It isn't much of a jump to see that presence is the same thing whether you call your passage a corporate career or a seeking journey.

So, What Is a Pointer?

A pointer is a statement with no claim to be true. Why is that? The entire purpose of a pointer is to deconstruct what you likely already hold as your go-to or default truth. Pointers help dissolve or drop the "bottom" out of the knee-jerk of your mind and deliver you into experience itself. Awakening is not an intellectual event. And you, yourself, are not an intellectual container, even though you may not believe it yet. You need pointers but working with them can be difficult. That's because they are such a different way of processing reality. And because they are new, even foreign, they can be challenging to remember. You are taking a new pointer into a lifetime of conditioning. So, pat yourself on the back and get on board and admit you will have bouts of amnesia now and then. Pointers take practice.

Pointers will also often seem so obvious. But blink and they all but slip out of your hands, time after time. Think of all of the arguments over the nature of the spiritual path. All of them are simply unnecessary, as the point of an argument is useless in the seeking. Why? Because in pointers there is no truth, nor is truth necessary. And yet we can find folks arguing in all corners of the world over pointers! Get it? Maybe not yet, but you will.

Again, a pointer is intended to awaken you to a behavior that is automatic and unconscious. Our behaviors are based on a story that at some point in time we accepted, likely innocently, and then stored and now that behavior happens with little or no thought. All of this unconscious behavior is centered around the assumption that we are an autonomous author of our own journey. That's right. The ego again. If awakening is the revelation that we are not an entity, but consciousness itself, then the continual unconscious imprinting of our ego-ness is counterproductive to say the least. Pointers are intended to surface the original story and then dissolve it by giving you a chance consciously to enter a new awakening story.

HERE IS A POINTER TO ILLUSTRATE.
IT IS CALLED "THE TEACUP TOO FULL"

A young seeker came to an ancient Zen master hoping to become a disciple. The master courteously invited him to join in having afternoon tea. As is typical in our talkative culture, the young man spoke throughout their entire teatime together, hardly leaving a moment for the old wiseman to comment. As they began their second cup, the master poured tea into the young man's cup but kept pouring and pouring and pouring until the cup was overrun. Tea spilled all over the table and puddled onto the floor. The young man screamed, "My teacup is too full! My teacup is too full!" He was aghast.

The master stopped and looked his guest squarely in the eyes. "Young man," he said, "you are like this cup. Brimming with so much that there is only one direction in which the tea can go. Please. Go home. Empty your cup. Once you have done that, you can return to me. Then we can consider your desire to become a disciple."

So, what is the "take home" from this pointer? We are conditioned to believe that we always have to have something to say. We incessantly deliver. We are the world's authorities on our own opinion, and we grasp every chance to let other folks know. Blah, blah, blah. We are teacups too full. Our ego, in its need to deliver, blocks any possibility to learn to be open, empty, to anything new.

Can't Get There from Here

I often use the pointer of the difference between water and wetness. What is the difference? One connotes a concept and the other experience. You say I am wet, not I am water. Most intellects will want to explore that difference in language and definition. But the sage knows that one well-placed swift kick can deliver the seeker into the water itself. So, while the intellectual version might focus on where the kick should be delivered and in how many foot-pounds, the mystic simply waits to hear the splash.

Some may claim that this commentary is anti-intellectual, but nothing could be further from the truth. It is actually the concepts themselves that undo other concepts that hold us in bondage. Intellect has its place, and when out of place or assumed to be all powerful simply cannot deliver outcomes. Ramana Maharshi used to compare concepts (intellect) to thorns. He would say that it takes one thorn to dig out another. Then he would point out that once extracted, both thorns should be thrown away. Just as a hammer is perfect for a nail, it's not often used to repair glass.

When I was a child one of my favorite black and white TV shows was Abbott and Costello. Perhaps one of my most enduring memories is in one skit where Abbot asks Costello directions to a destination. Costello immediately and sadly replies, "You can't get there from here". I remember my father found this response to be of the highest order of humor. I can still hear him cackling at the comment. But as a child, that reply made perfect sense. It seemed possible that this could be true.

Which of these two views is the correct one? My father saw humor because his story, and that of most experienced folks, is that one can get anywhere from anywhere else. An adult comedian is a perfect ruse to make fun of what an adult doesn't think possible. A child hasn't learned that. He sees no issue that there are places one can't get to from anywhere else. Places for him include the possibility that one can't be reached from here or anywhere for that matter. So, both stories can claim to be true. And the world map will appear differently depending on which story is operational. The pointer that 'you can't get there from here' might live perfectly in experience to create a certain outcome. But adults everywhere will argue that it is entirely incorrect.

SAGE OR ACADEMIC?
POINTERS NOT CONCEPTS

In a nutshell, the penetration into the illusion of meaning is precisely the difference between a sage and an academic. Embedded in the rigor of academia are assumptions that mystics simply ignore. Why? The sage's thrust is to propel the seeker into the pool of being, unceremoniously or otherwise. The academic seems to believe that concepts can be honed and delivered in some better or more pure form than others. And once done, this tour de force is celebrated as meaningful in some way. This obviously ignores that meaning itself relies on separation, as it is a distant extraction leaving behind all that does not contribute to itself. It is an illusion.

The awakened mystic, when reduced to intellectual discourse, hopes to find a way by utilizing concepts as pointers to the territory of being itself. The ejection of the seeker from the illusionary map of separation and into consciousness itself is the sole occupation of the sage. Make no mistake here. A sage may use anything to create the awakening outcome. There are no ethics in awakening!

What is the difference between a concept or story and presence itself? The entire seekers' trek on the path of wisdom is cast by this one shift from intellect to tangible reality. You see, we have both learned and been conditioned to believe that an intellectual notion, story or concept is tangible reality. But presence lives in prior unity to the separating activity which is that of the intellect. The path of knowledge is the domain of all that is intellectually processed and rendered.

What you are and the awakening to that is the ground zero of pointers. This ground zero lives prior to your assumption that concept is reality. Whenever we attach ourselves to an intellectual claim, we have stopped short of engaging our presence and, yes, giving consciousness a chance to reveal itself as who you really are. The result of this identification with concept is to remain in the conflation, or even superimposition, of story on to the presence which lies below. This is one of the toughest distinctions to keep present in our travels as everything we have learned, and that which is held in the main collective of our own humanity, revels in this conflation.

The awkward conversation between seeker and sage is

largely carried on in two operational stories that actually collide. The sage sees from the perspective of "all that is" and delivers his commentary from the active emergence of that revelation. Meanwhile, the seeker knows only to cobble together pieces of life's manifestation and assumes that construction is equal to what the mystic sees. But you can't get there from here. The ocean of consciousness informs its own emergence and is not in the realm of equivalence with intellect. One is true cognition from being to conceptual output while the other is the construction of smog particulates claiming to be fresh air. For this reason, awakening is a traffic pattern of pointers and presence, not concepts that could ever be declared true or superior to another.

RAMESH AND THE ARGENTINIAN MAN

As you can readily see by this last paragraph, the simple exposition of a pointer can be tough slogging. That's the bad news. The good news is that we both encounter and engage with this in our felt experience daily. Here is a humorous experience of that collision in a Ramesh Balsekar Satsang where I was called into action.

Ramesh's residence in Mumbai was mainly composed of two outer rooms where seekers could congregate during his discourse. One of those was a smaller space where Ramesh sat. Those of us who frequented the gatherings knew that this room was where the first-time visitors would be lovingly placed. It held about 12 people comfortably. Additionally, there was a large living room in which a diligent volunteer who recorded each days' speaking did his job. In the corner of the large room sat a metal garden swing, the kind that ubiquitously appears in the backyards of homes throughout the world. It was well known that I loved to sit in this swing with my eyes shut as I simply absorbed the Satsang wave.

It was during one of those humid October days while in my swinging happy place, that I was jerked into action as Ramesh loudly called out my name. Not only was this unusual, but it was also unprecedented. I couldn't imagine why he would need me as I made my way into the small room.

Apparently, an older gentleman from Argentina had come to that day's Satsang. He didn't speak a word of English and yet seem compelled to deliver an important message to Ramesh. He wanted Ramesh to understand that God as a concept was both alive and the way home. Of course, Ramesh spent lavish amounts of time pointing out that by separating ourselves from God or consciousness and then attempting to claim unity of God and us as distinct objects led to a Groundhog Day style of a life of infinite regression. This was the source of seekership in the first place!

But before he could even address this seemingly complex issue, he had to surmount the larger obstacle of understanding a man who only spoke Spanish. That is where I came in! Ramesh, of course, knew that I spoke fluent Spanish both from my missionary times as a Mormon missionary in Peru and in my business career shuttling into and out of the various Spanish speaking countries. He called me to translate. Luckily, I thrust myself into the task at hand. I am sure I would have otherwise fainted at the thought of translating a conversation about seeking from or into any language that I knew if I hadn't been absorbed into the very moment. You see business and street speak is not typically the stuff of pointing to consciousness!

Nonetheless, here I was lucky enough to witness the collision between the belief in a concept and the utilization of the concept as a true pointer to awakening. For this beautiful Argentinian man had come all this way to deliver to Ramesh what he felt was the only true concept of awakening. His belief was the commonly held version. A true concept can be rendered in language. Of course, Ramesh spent a lifetime pointing at this common and ubiquitous misconception. It cannot.

Ramesh, in his own ruthless clarity, spoke to this man. He said, "This is my concept. It is in no way meant to compete with any other concept. Its only use is as a pointer to something beyond concept itself. You obviously believe that by coming and straightening me out, as it were, that some great good will be served. But that would be a colossal waste of time. If you believe that the perfect concept needs to be delivered for awakening to occur and that such an exercise is a competitive venture, then you should give your own Satsang where great ideas can struggle and win. But here concepts operate as pointers and this is the basic agreement of my gatherings."

Wow. In all of this, both men sat smiling at one another.

Nonetheless, here we see the collision of a well-meaning ego crashing into the nothingness of the mystic. Our Argentinian was a sweet man attempting to make life a more stable place by codifying and concretizing a teaching. There ultimately is no place to find sure footing in the "out there" of manifestation. That is because stable rooting is only in pure awareness, which underpins the faded version of intellectual concept that seeks to take its place. Consciousness is the principle of tangible movement and activity. Awareness is its birther and that is only found within. This first pointer is such an act of compassion to take the seeker off the hook of looking for awakening where it will never be found.

So, as you come to believe that you have found it, whatever it is, ask yourself "Is this a story or concept that lives on the outside?" If it is, throw it away. For beyond that false destination awaits a wisdom that comes here and now. It passes through us as a conduit, an activity that only presence can generate. Often one doesn't even know what will pass through, yet simply stands on the stage, that isn't a stage, speaking what wants and needs to be spoken. This is the standing in consciousness or presence that I speak of in a never-ending way. Why? When all one has known is the imposition of separate story obscuring the presence underneath, the steadfast stance in this pointer will break the programming of the single track of intellect.

And remember, as you onboard the pointers and read, listen, even imbibe the stories, that this is all simply my concept or story, if you will. It is entirely generated from consciousness itself as driven through some character called Alan. It has no use as a participant in an intellectual contest nor does it seek to be named a winner of any kind. It does intend to deliver a footprint to the posterior of readers such that they end up wet. I am listening for the splash.

part one

Pointers to Awakening

chapter one

————•◦ ⚬◯⚬ ◦•————

The wisdom path

WELCOME to the new terrain I call "The Wisdom Path". Pointers are one of the main devices that you will encounter along your way. They will help you return to your original birthright that you always have held, but likely forgot was even there. These pointers have no intention of being true, which is a measurement in the path of knowledge, but not on the wisdom path. There are so many differences between the two. I will take you through a bit of both in the hopes that you will begin to acclimate and then embrace the wisdom path in your own life journey. But first let's talk about the basis of the wisdom world itself. It all centers around intuition. Intuition is not a memory but an inbuilt dog tag of the identification of your original self. It is the magnetic north that pulls the spiritual path towards home.

An old Indian story tells of a time that God gathered all of creation and said, "I want to hide the gift of wisdom from humans until they are ready for it. For it is the awakening that they may then have an authentic place in my manifestation. Once found this wisdom will give them permanent peace."

The hawk chimed in first, "Give it to me; I'll fly to the moon and bury it there."

But God said, "No, one day they will go there and will find it."

Then the shark, "Give it to me; I'll carry it in the depths of the ocean."

"No," said God, "they'll get there too."

Then the buffalo offered, "Give it to me; I'll hide it in our dung."

Again, God said, "No, they will get there. Finally, the Ancient Mother in the form of a mole came. She did not have the eyes to see in the normal fashion but had the inner eye. She said, "Put it in their intuition on the inside. They'll never find it there."

And the God said, "Let it be".

As you know this book is an invitation to presence. Intuition and presence are a connected duo. Presence is the always present awareness that is in your entire life. You were there as the same thing for your 5-year-old happenings, your 25-year-old happenings and your 65-year-old happenings. That awareness is your felt presence. Intuition is the exclusive internal broadcaster, the NBC, BBC or YouTube of presence as it were. If presence were FIFA, the NFL or Downtown Abbey you could only find them on the exclusive broadcaster called the intuition channel. When you accept the invitation to presence just RSVP to your intuition.

Now here is an obvious question. What has happened to that intuition? It is arguably our first and most powerful gift. Where is it? This originally installed human accessory is a place we now hide things and are hidden from. What happened? Traditional approaches to transformation and awakening have taken the tack of looking at a conditioned personality, the story identity, as if they are the layers of an onion. They start with the concept that a human being is a construction of parts, known as conditioning, and that each layer should be treated one at a time. The way to move to the central essence of the individual in this paradigm is to peel these layers, one at a time. These parts represent the conditioning of 'woulds', 'coulds', and 'shoulds' that have been acquired since the birth of the body mind. I often call this the bastardization of your original Self. As is the case of all upbringings, these parts have been acquired through Santa's helpers - the culture, society, parents, teachers, clergy, government and institutions. And climbing down into the layers is typically labeled is an 'outside-in' method. It is easy to see why this is the case.

In this conditioning process, each of us has been taught that we are our story. We identify with it totally. This teaching induces us to conflate story, an intellectual holding, with presence and consciousness. In so doing we are also taught to largely ignore the co-opted prior unity of presence. Remember, it has been and always is there. Intuition is the advisory of movement towards our original self at the deepest level. It is synonymous with presence and consciousness for the most part.

This onion method focuses on one piece of conditioning at a time. First, one identifies with the conditioning. Secondly, one moves to the recognition that the conditioning is not who one truly is. And in the recognition that what had been previously thought to be a permanent part of you, the possibility arises that the new you minus this 'issue' is a step toward transformation. Often this approach is accompanied by meditation, for in the silence it is easier to identify what may not be you when your active conditioning is not in play. Of course, this path continues as long as one thinks that they are an individual composed of a variety of layers of conditioning which in some order need to be identified. Then each piece is dropped when it is seen not to be part of the individual. In other words, one never moves beyond the identified ego when only dealing with its ornaments and not the ego itself.

The problem with this approach is that much like creating a mosaic in the beach sand, the conditionings that are left behind are so voluminous that they tumble downward to fill in the hole. Yes, it looks like every time a piece is extracted that the new mosaic forms a new picture. But after a time, it is easy to see that the granules are innumerable. And the feeling that it is impossible to extract enough of the granules to actually arrive at any new depth is rife. It can be disheartening as it seems that the new pieces of conditioning are stacked in a never-ending line. They act like customers taking a number at a great ice cream parlor. The ego as the ticket taker finds that there is infinite line of life issues holding their number wanting their flavor of today's ice cream!

With this approach comes the felt experience of consciousness as a subset of the mind or intellect. Because the pieces are defined concepts held in the mind, the action is always outside-in. This approach leads one to believe that intellect does in some way hold wisdom and maybe even directs it. Sadly, it doesn't do either. But consider for just a moment the story that you, yourself, are simply an ego composition that has been extracted from consciousness itself. You are a concept all in one piece, a really big single concept. And all of these conditionings are simply ornaments or attachments to the first moment of 'I am' or birth.

Does this create an easier way? If one could simply stand in the essence of 'I am' and ask that simple question "Who is aware of that 'I am?'" then all the examinations of distant conditionings could simply be circumvented. Instead of becoming aware of each appendage hanging off the ego, now one becomes aware of the ego itself in its earliest purity.

Now, to return to the peeling of the onion metaphor, each of the 'woulds', 'coulds', and 'shoulds' are simply extracted through the process of cognition. But the biggest extraction, that we constantly rearrange and gussy up, is our ego itself. I call the peeling the onion approach, the indirect approach. For if all we are doing is dissolving concepts held in the assumptive state, the necessity of dissolving them one at a time is clearly indirect. As the sand of the mosaic rushes in, it has to become obvious that we will never reach the ego itself. But if we know that all of the onion layer concepts are inherently connected and hang off one concept called ego, why wouldn't we simply look at that primal ego assumption? This inquiry is what I deem the direct approach. And the direct approach is inside-out. The felt experience of this wisdom approach is entirely different as well. It is not a mental experience of managing parts into reality, but rather experiencing reality itself as it created the one thing you are in the ego form.

Let's use surfing, one of my favorite experiences, as an example. The beginning surfer normally holds certain beliefs. They believe that they are in charge of the surfing experience, waves and all. They also believe that they can take certain small pieces of the experience, foot placement, the proper wax, you name it, and manage the perfect ride. But this approach is mental, and the experience cannot become a wholistic flow. Approaching surfing from the outside-in only takes one so far. We could call this the indirect method of surfing!

But there is a bridge to a land of wisdom that lies beyond the fractured pieces approach. Many of these early surfers begin to recognize this mental limitation and, many times with the help of a mentor, begin to see surfing as an emergence which includes them as the surfer. In this new learning they begin to feel how they are simply carried by much larger forces than themselves. They are indeed just a small part of the whole thing. This moment is a felt experience of a different class. It is a perfect flow and the possibility is to allow all that surrounds and includes the surfer to produce the emergence of the highest possibility of peace. And a good ride. Many surfers spend their entire life seeking this exact moment.

For seekers, much like surfers, we surf the waves of life

in one of two positions. In the first we believe we are moving towards mastery and that our ego will subdue and finally hold control over the wave we surf. We think that we can become a stable, immovable object of perfect non-motion on the wildest wave the ocean of life can serve up. The second is the recognition that what lies within the motion of life itself is the place for which we are authentically designed. It is that perfect motion, embedded in the larger movement of motion, that is akin to the still point of permanent stability. That perfect stability is within the motion itself. All that has to happen is the surrender of the autonomous assumption we continuously make about our ego self. Have you ever been in the perfect flow and one with a wave? If so, you have had a free sample of the wisdom path.

You see, the gift of wisdom lives on the inside and is unleashed by movement from the inside-out. All of our lifetime learning has unwittingly told us exactly the opposite. We have been taught to learn things and hold them in the mind inserting them piece by piece into reality to change the whole. The wisdom path is finding the gift on the inside. That is where intuition has been telling you it is all along. And the confirmation is the difference in how it feels when wisdom is in play. As long as we believe that we, as an ego, could be in control the highest possibility attainable is that of ego self-mastery. That possibility is an illusion. As this illusion is seen through there lies the bridge to wisdom.

The Knowledge Path is not the Wisdom Path

You likely are asking yourself why I go to such length in the revelation of wisdom versus knowledge as paths of felt experiences. Until now, most have never even thought of that difference. In our life we have been taught that knowledge is the only learning goal. You have a problem? Great, go get some knowledge. There then comes a time when a recognition arises that tells you that there is more in the learning process than just information. Now, life becomes more about the journey than the destination. Still, however, most of us continue to go get knowledge rather than develop a way of approaching the seasoning of life in a unique way. It is the nature of being human to attempt to move through new experience by repeating what one has always done. Remember the old saying, "When all you have is a hammer, the entire world looks like a nail"?

In 1987 I realized that it was time to begin my own search. I had checked every box of achievement that I had been told was necessary to be a success. And yet I was miserable internally and knew that there must be something missing. At the time, I was at the zenith of my corporate career and beyond wildly successful. But for all that, I still was familiar only with the approaches to development that I had seen in my education and career. As I undertook to find out about anything spiritual, I came up with little or nothing. I simply didn't know how to find or even understand the resources I would need to move forward.

First, I attacked the metaphysical bookstores. It was not unusual to find me sitting on the floor in the aisle of a bookstore with stacks of books around me. This would go on until the staff would politely ask me to leave as they turned out the lights at closing. I did find a lot of what I was looking for in print but still I knew very few folks who had ever been a spiritual seeker. This, of course, was in an era of no internet. Nonetheless, finding the information was only a small bit of my undertaking. My search blossomed into years in India and sitting at the feet of enlightened masters. I suppose, since I had found mentors in my corporate career, I intuitively knew to find mentors, as it were, in my search. Although resources are easier to find now, the understanding of the nature of this journey is still hard to find. My entire passion in writing this book is to introduce the seeker to the terrain and the experience of walking through it. I care deeply that this is available for those who wish to understand.

I think the best way to tackle this subject is to compare what you already know to the new version you will need to undertake and remember. You know the approach of acquiring knowledge. I will link the components of that process to the wisdom path.

The first thing to recognize is that you likely have spent your entire life centered around a belief that the intellect is the solver of all life issues. Yet, what has you even engaged in this search? You feel something internal that tells you there is more than meets the eye in your life until now. That sense is so strong that you are in action as a result.

This is your intuition speaking to you. When I first felt this, I did what most would do. I jumped right back into my intellectual search for knowledge. Intuition is the ruler of the wisdom path, whereas the intellect is the ruler of knowledge. Intuition lies in the preverbal space between consciousness or presence itself and the story that you have always believed that you are. Going back into that story will give you no relief. Your intuition is the essence of your true self. It is messaging to you that you have arrived at an in-authentic destination, your story or fake self. This fake self is the story that has resulted from a lifetime of "woulds', "shoulds', and 'coulds". This story identity is your genuine response in reaction to your upbringing to be what everyone wanted you to be.

You now need to trek back to your original face and find out how you might emerge. What will emerge? The "original myth" self or the true self. Why can't intellect do the heavy lifting here? Think about it for a moment. The intellect is, by nature, an activity in separation. Its job is to extract from all that is particular pieces and process them. Wisdom, on the other hand, arises from "prior unity". That is to say that you, as a being, are not separate from all that is. Where can you find this sense? It is in your intuition. In spiritual circles this sense is often referred to as the "I am." It is pure being which broadcasts out as pure presence. The rise of presence is simply your perfect and original self being lived by consciousness. That perceptive frame is effusive. It broadcasts itself. When folks say they have been in the presence of greatness that is simply them feeling the synchronous unity of their own presence with that of another. Ultimately this unity includes all of consciousness. That is the spiritual trek, to trace back to that place where you, as your story self, left the barn of consciousness. This is the intuitive exercise of the wisdom path. In essence we get to use our intellectual construction process of building a story in an entirely new way. We are using the intellect to dissolve itself rather than build more of its kingdom. Yep, it's a "going backwards" exercise.

In short, the spiritual journey intends to dissolve your pre-conceived assumptions and avoid replacing them. This leaves you in a conceptless and storyless world of being which is who you really are. How do we do this? I will point you to a world where intellectual constructions simply don't live. What does live in that world? Why, consciousness itself!

How will you know that you are moving in the wisdom path? You will notice that instead of truth, that you will be seeking revelation. Truth is a fictitious positing of the intellect in the world of knowledge. Revelation is the outpouring of consciousness, not of the mind. You will notice that competition isn't a help in your movement, rather collaboration is the stuff that leads you back home. You have always believed in facts. What are facts? They are pieces of intellectual separation that supposedly are better than other pieces. What does that get you but a position in an argument that you feel is superior? Now you will be using pointers. A pointer, again, is an intellectual signpost pointing to something before and beyond itself. It points to being. It points to presence. Being is not a destination like a fact but a tangible sense of self. In short, the intellectual will be complicit in replacing itself with tangibility. What will this tangibility give you? It will deliver a felt sense of permanent and perfect peace internally.

The wisdom path is an iterative one. That is to say that the very same pointer can be used over and over again as one penetrates the mystery of being. The linear approach to accumulating the content of knowledge will not be of any use. The point of the knowledge path is to advance to a higher level of held facts and truth. The point of the wisdom path is to rest in being in such a way that presence rises through and with you. You will notice yourself often using your knowledge approach unconsciously as that is what we have been conditioned to do for a lifetime. To sink into the consciousness that you are and perceive the revelation of what is turns out to be tougher than one might imagine. We have never been introduced to simply being.

Perhaps the biggest noticing will be the difference between tension and relaxation. Whether you have noticed it or not (and I invite you to) the knowledge path in its natural separative approach requires tension to manage all these supposed facts and truth. The wisdom path and awakening are entirely a relaxation. Relaxing into all that is. Watching the construction of your assumptions dissolve. Now back to iterative.

What do I mean by iterative? Let me tell you one of my stories from my longish career. In my younger days I was privileged to be in a process group of CEOs. There were 14 of us and we would meet for a whole day once a month to be a working board of directors to each other. Now, I was just 29 at the time having rocketed into success at a very young age. Around me sat "long time" executives of household name companies. Over the 5 years we were together these men became my dearest friends, but early on I was still clearly the puppy of the group.

On one of these early days, we were asked to go around the room and point out the most powerful attribute of each CEO. Of course, all of the seasoned leaders were easy to classify. But when they got to me you could see this room of executives was clearly at a loss as to what to say. In fact, they were uncomfortable. Finally, one of the men said, "I think Alan's most powerful personal attribute is the ability to make the obvious more so." This, of course, threw the room into a fit of laughter as we all were now off the uncomfortable hook. Now, years later, I see that this story is exactly the case. The simplicity of the obvious is the wisdom that often is overlooked due to its very simplicity.

Many readers might now say "But I am not in business, what could this mean for something much more important like the spiritual journey?" Guess what? Iterative means the same pointer only acting every time in a more profound way. Every time I read my own writing I want to scream. There is only one thing to know. We live in a state of misidentification. Every, and I mean every, pointer is dedicated to dissolving, obliterating and shattering that false story. That's it. No matter what, don't lose your contact with that one understanding. That was the secret to my journey. When I heard Osho talk about the ego, I knew he knew. I was on a plane to India 4 weeks later. When Ramesh Balsekar told me to hold on to the "I Am", as it was my true story, that never left my intention. It was shortly after this that my awakening story on the 405-freeway occurred. That shift has been permanent since 1999 and the apperception of my true self has continued to this day. Nisargadatta called it earnestness. I call it "making the obvious more so".

When you enter a new context or territory you must learn how to tread its paths. You will find that you use your old approach, that of intellect and knowledge, in approaching the new context time and time again. Worry not. It is like riding a bike. Get back on every time you fall off. After a time, you will fall less. The reason it is important for you to know the difference is to broaden your perception such that a new discipline will emerge that has you imbedded in the wisdom path. That is your true self. You may remember an old saying that goes, "What got you here, won't get you there". This will be the biggest version of that saying you will ever undertake.

chapter two

——•◦ ⚬ ◦•——

The Invitation into presence

I WANT TO START WITH an invitation. It is a deeply personal one, but also points to the feeling that likely has you reading a seekers' book. You know that there is something out there, and something inside that just doesn't work. Something doesn't feel right in yourself and in your life. You aren't the first. It doesn't matter how far you go back in history, the fabric of humanity, as perceived by millions of well-intentioned or not so well-intentioned souls, is that something feels wrong. There is sense we are not seeing all that there is.

I was dipped in this water of wanting to know from an early age. And what came with it was an experience of presence and the power of story. I invite you to enjoy and even live in my experience.

The younger years of a child's life can hold the most indelible parts of what later will become an adult life. This has to be magnified when a grandfather of depth and presence is along for the ride. In fact, I could say that my life has been a series of relationships with people whose felt presence has always enveloped me. I have been asked many times "What is presence?" I reach for the words that usually pour out more in story form, but in the end, presence is a felt experience of magnetic essence. Much like speaking about water and hoping to understand "wet", presence is being.

Most of us believe that anything can be held and conveyed in words. But is that true? Check your own experience on this one. One of the first and foremost lessons from my grandfather was to examine experience and see that there was indeed a world prior to language. In fact, the entire proposition of the writing of mankind has been to attempt, as best as possible, to capture the felt experience of perception with the frame of words or intellect. Ultimately, there is a gap that simply cannot be crossed. Words are just pointers and no matter how magnificent they are, that is their limitation.

It is in the spiritual journey that this recognition is found. The conflation of being and intellectual structure are teased out and held in the reverence they deserve, once seen. What does this have to do with my grandpa? Intuitively he recognized this gap and rooted me for a lifetime in presence. Think of the myriad of ways we attempt to describe this rooted sense. We call it being, being at hand, in the moment, tangibility, visceral and on and on. We attempt to describe this principle of action. It is the juice of being, it percolates up, it locates in the spine or maybe the third eye. But in the end the only hope of all of this descriptive is that a living understanding will develop wherein the pointer migrates into experience. Presence is why the word ineffable was created. The attempt to describe what cannot be described, only experienced. Again, the gap! Are you tired of all of this? Great, here is my pointer, meet my Grandpa.

Most everyone called my grandpa "Ed". He was about 5'8", so not especially imposing. At least not in physical stature. A northern Californian of some generations, he loved reading Charles Dickens, all kinds of philosophy, and quoting Irish limericks. In my younger years, Grandpa loved to smoke a pipe. The cherry flavors wafted through the air and seemed stuck, especially in his study. Oh, his study! It was our place. Books on the wall, leather chairs and things that he loved. What do Grandpa's love? His pipes stood on a carousel next to his model of a 1957 Pontiac Chieftain. He had a steering wheel propped in the corner of the room and it was intended to be touched by any and all children. He had statues of giraffes and elephants. The elephants quickly increased their herd size when it was discovered that they were my favorites.

Imagine a childhood in the 50's in which the mystery of anything would be tackled. For most men, their study belongs only to them. Grandpa's study was an invitation to his grandchildren. Forays to the beach, park, zoo and kitchen raids were all sourced from the study. And he had maps, boy did he have maps. It was common to find us in that place with maps of anywhere in the world, but especially California, spread out to cover anything that had the misfortune of usurping the adventure space. These physical elements were the props for profound, unforgettable, wisdom moments. But they were just props. The main attraction was the simple possibility of being with Grandpa!

When I was quite young, I began crawling into my Grandfather's lap. In that warmth and connection, I heard teaching stories that touched me deeply. He didn't read them, rather he passed them on in our own inside oral tradition. This tradition had curiosity as its trademark. But the deeper contract that we shared together was to always look beyond whatever narrative we encountered. A story is never just a story. My Grandfather used to love to tell me *The Emperor's New Clothes*. Here is a little synopsis to remind you of the obvious plot.

Long ago and far away there lived an Emperor who considered himself to possess the finest attributes of taste and class. His city's principal purpose was to set the public stage so that he could be seen and applauded. When it came to his attire, the finest designers of the moment were at his beck and call to create a wardrobe of unique and unrepeatable fashions. Once created, the Emperor spared no time in playing peacock.

It was into this world that one of the finest designers was summoned. He was called "magical" and "beyond compare." It was said that it took the finest eye to even perceive the perfection of his designs. In fact, he would take sketches to his clients which often appeared to be simply blank sheets of paper. But time and time again there would be a small group, led by the Emperor, who claimed they could see the colors and feel the texture of the remarkable garments. And although they would tour the tailor's room, it appeared to many that cloth and thread were truly invisible. Of course, they all assumed their own lack of seeing was a mistake and a reflection of their own lack of class and taste.

The Emperor was so excited by this new designer that he vowed to hold a parade in which the entire kingdom would attend. Sure enough, that the day arrived, and every resident bathed and dressed in their Sunday best, with anticipation and fanfare. The Emperor made his way down the main street, and as he neared the center of town, there stood a father with his young son on his shoulders craning his head to get the absolute best view. When the boy saw the Emperor, he simply couldn't hold it in and gushed "The Emperor has no clothes! The Emperor has no clothes!"

Now, my grandpa would say we don't know exactly what happened after that moment. Maybe the Emperor carried on pretending and demanding that all pretend with him. Or maybe he, too, saw the unveiling for what it was and ran terrified back to the palace. But we do know that this moment was marked as the most important and was recited in annals for centuries to come. In fact, it was many a philosopher and storyteller who would weave this great human foible into their deliveries.

My grandpa said when folks hold rigidly to any version of reality or perception there needs to be skepticism. He also shared that illusion depends on self-deception and ignorance. While he was compassionate, people often could not accept the clarity he might have expressed. Clarity, in today's world, simply isn't politically correct. Now, as a boy I may not have understood the teachings of the story of the Emperor all that well. But this experience of story holding clarity as a teaching device became part of the fabric that was Grandpa and me. Eventually it got easier for me to see that humans clothe themselves in all kinds of story but that in the end the story falls off and all is left is the nakedness of consciousness itself. Hopefully, that is. As Grandpa used to say, "How can you be the story when you can see it from afar?" What then, are you really?

Stories were always in large supply. We talked of butterflies, with one even named Norman, as easily as the most famous characters in history. This is where I first heard about Socrates. Socrates, my grandpa told me, had the habit of gathering little ones like me around him and letting them ask questions. At the center of Socrates' effort was the passion to have each of the children be present. Present? Yep, that was Grandpa's word for being there at hand. With his grandchild, Grandpa had the liberty of touch and embrace. He could hold my little body as easily as he could hold my gaze. Then he would connect his physicality and tangibility to the story he would tell. So many times, I would hear "Chuck, it's like this when you know" as he lovingly grazed my shoulder or the side of my cheek. It was from this essence that I felt like I knew Socrates, and I was sure my grandpa did. Yes, Grandpa called me Chuck rather than Alan. It was a name I simply chose, and we agreed. Easy.

It was only years later that I discovered that Socrates did not teach young ones at all. In fact, he was much more of a professor than the pied piper of questioning children like my grandpa had made him out to be. Now, most folks would be dismayed at the molding that this story had taken at the hands of the man I loved. But not me. Our stories always had room for change and transformation. I realized that a wise man with a beloved child in his lap lets the story meet the child himself. A wise man teaches what needs to be learned. You see, wisdom and presence and story are perfect mates. My grandfather created the feeling of wise presence in every story he told. Sitting in his lap listening and feeling his presence, well, it helped me discover mine.

chapter three

—•⊙ ༘⊙༘ ⊙•—

LIKE A FISH IN WATER

IN SOME WAYS humans are quite predictable. We wander around with a myriad of questions about who we are, meanwhile, we rarely take notice that our perception is actually creating that world of questions itself. What is the deepest possibility of human experience? Who am I really? How does one undertake the journey to answer this question? Pointers are an approach in service of these inquiries. And no matter whether an approach is expressed in stories, prose, or intellectual conceptual models, it is not only about its style, but also about how close its proximity is to the emergent nature of consciousness itself.

Since the beginning of time, humans have found themselves part of an ongoing emergence of manifestation. The response to this position has been to develop a frame that places humans in some relationship to everything else. We can occupy the center, the perimeter, even be part of the interconnected whole. Even the so-called whole of interconnectedness is consistently described as an amalgamation of pieces. But in the frame of intellectual extraction, contrast is a necessity. In order to talk about us, no matter our stated context, humans are separately considered in any theory of humanity. In fact, human cognition is simply a rendering of some phenomenon into a meaningful frame.

Many refer to this ultimately automatic action as "meaning-making". And indeed, it is. But in so doing, humans have assumed the sense of separation into their very cognition. For contrast is simply another word for separation. It is only by seeing one thing separate from another that contrast can be said to exist. And thus, began humanity's first assumption that being is located in separate human entities roughly defined by the perceivable physical body. When did they decide that each one of these physical bodies was autonomously authoring their own journey? I suspect fairly immediately.

But is this who we really are? For the entirety of human history as we have it, the inquiry into "Who Am I?" has been ongoing. In fact, history has offered up a variety of versions of what this "I" might be. Clearly no credit has ever been given for the arrival at the actual understanding of what we are. We are still arguing about it. Thousands of years ago, astrology and pantheistic religion sought to locate the assumed individual "I" within a story of particulars. Today these systems are seen as superstitious tripe. They have been replaced with quantum mechanics, string theory and monotheistic religion. And someday all of these will move into that same arena of superstitious tripe. What is really going on? We don't know who we are.

That is what I am saying. The one thing common to human experience and thought is the assumption that we know who we are. The fact we do not, has not stopped us for one minute in developing all of the rest of our stories and theories dependent on that first unknown, long given up. We simply align our new supposed knowledge around an assumption that we do know who we are, when in fact, we really do not. But this is much like introducing a zero into your last multiplication formula and then pretending that the result of your equation actually is a whole number. A whole number must be multiplied by another whole number in order for your equation to produce a tangible result. However, when a zero is introduced in the multiplication process it renders the result a zero as well. It doesn't matter how many whole numbers there are in addition to the zero. One is all it takes. The difference between a mathematician and the average person is that for the mathematician the zero cannot be denied. Not knowing what exactly is meant by "I" and yet assuming that one does in every ongoing activity is simply denying that the zero is in the process. It is assumptive both in thought and in experience.

Intellect Is Not Experience Itself

One unseen or ignored assumption does seem to lead to more. It is like pretending your weed garden is actually full of lilies. So how can story help us in ways that the intellectual development of theories and models has not been able to deliver for thousands of years? First let's take a look at some of the other assumptions we have made along our historical way. One of the most pervasive is that there is some truth or arrival point to which our intellect can deliver us. But is that true? Does life really happen in the intellectual conclusions that we draw while in the phenomenal flow of life itself? I would clearly propose that this is not the case, and I would be in a historical minority. Every day we see human conflict arranged around which one of the multiple intellectual conclusions are true. And that conflict is based on an assumption. And because of that assumption we worship intellectual conclusions over the simple occurrence of activity that happens daily in front of our face.

And what is that occurrence of activity? It is story. And story itself, for many, must arrive at a conclusion. But this is just the leakage of our intellectual holding into the essence of story itself. Has your story really ever ended? If you are reading this sentence, you might notice that if you raise your eyes that it's happening much like it always has. Your story has no beginning, and it has no end. You actually know that tangibly. Life as it emerges, once cognized, is simply an incessant thread of story. And if your story has conclusions and outcomes then you have simply punctuated the flow. You have utilized your intellectual capability to induce contrast by placing convenient markers at different places to deliver conclusions.

Have you done this knowingly? That is a great question. Most likely you have simply on-boarded the learned grammatical holding of those around you and placed that into your own story creation. And without noticing, you have become one of those that worship intellectual insertion. This all sounds anti-intellectual to most of humanity. But it is similar to taking a dangerous item from your child and then being labeled anti-child. Intellect has an important place in experience, but it is not experience itself.

POINTERS HELP ERADICATE ASSUMPTIONS

Pointers utilize intellect, but in a much different way than our historical assumptions. A pointer is simply an invitation to change the frame of extraction that assumptively lives in your cognitive function. Years ago, Ramana Maharshi would quip that pointers and concepts are really like thorns. Using one thorn to pull out another was their very purpose. But most have forgotten what he said to do once the extraction had taken place. He implored us all to then throw the thorns away. Why? Because he knew that our intellectual traditions would have us puncture the old wound with the new thorn because we thought there should be at least one embedded at all times.

Pointers are for seekers that have begun to understand the futility of their own conclusions. So, what's next? An inquiry into the actual arising of experience can replace the conclusions that have been deemed somehow to represent it. And why story? If intellectual conclusions are a distant reflection of experience itself, then how can one penetrate that experience? If you think about your own life you will immediately find that stories, while cognized, retain much of the essence of experience itself. Stories hold the emotional field, the movement, and the immediacy of a cognized thread of life. Where could one go to begin an experiential movement toward the inquiry of "Who am I?" Story is the place that one could begin.

Now, Listen to the Story:

In a small village, many years back, there lived an old man who was a master in the art of teaching how to ride a bicycle. He was so successful that his students emerged looking like world class riders. It wasn't their speed; it was their presence. They rode so well and with such little effort that a rumor began to fly. Aha. There must be something magical in this old man's teaching. Everyone speculated as to what that might be. Soon this small village was renowned throughout the entire country as the center for perfection in bicycle riding.

One day, the word got out that the master would be teaching an 11-year-old girl the secrets of riding. Journalists and other interested folks rushed to the small village. The following morning the main street for the much-anticipated lesson was lined shoulder to shoulder with eager spectators. The girl appeared on her bike. There was a hush. And what did they see that day? They saw an old man run behind this girl yelling "Lean to the left! Lean to the left!" The following day the major newspaper blasted a big headline: "Bicycle Secret Exposed. Lean to the Left". Within a few short weeks several new books on bicycling premiered, all announcing "Lean to the Left" in their titles.

It must be apparent that the spectators and the news media missed the entire point of the old man's teaching. What was he really trying to accomplish? Balance. He was trying to bring his student into balance. There was no hidden secret. It was simply knowing what the truth was.

As you can see this story/pointer is intended to "out you" as it were. Here I talk about leaning to the left. But what happens if you need to lean to the right? Bingo. The pointer is not about where you lean but, rather, that you adjust from where you are. Again, pointers help you on the road to awareness and to the wisdom of presence, of consciousness beyond ego identification. Since everyone is on a different place on the path, the thrust of a pointer demands the flexibility of context. What is this pointer attempting to dissolve in your automatic, unconscious behavior? Let's first make an observation.

How do we really think? When we look for answers or solutions, we have the habit of grabbing on to the "one size fits all" version. We shouldn't be surprised. As children, our educational system placed a premium on grasping the one true answer. And we wanted to do it quickly, to keep pace with the demands of a curriculum that had certain 'learning' expectations.

How many times do we miss the point by employing our lifetime habit of grasping the so-called quick answer so we can keep pace? Think of the difference between being and doing. Doing has the component of speed and thus we can place a premium on getting there first. Then once there we rarely, if ever, revisit. Why would we? We have the right answer. But in being there is no speed. It simply is here and now with no descriptors.

Watch your mind as you move through your own journey and you will be surprised how often your mind rushes to get to the answer. This is now long held, automatic behavior. It is a deep habit. Period. But since you are unconscious so much of the time to what is 'really' happening, when you try to change your habits and patterns, your mind will explode into a 5-bell alert! Why? Because behind the scenes, the mind is always tracking how the happenings on the outside fit its story, even when the story is not useful or true.

So, pointers dissolve our long held, unexamined stories, those that have obfuscated what can be revealed with a deeper understanding. We could call that deeper understanding the actual thrust of the matter. So, consider, if you believe you grasp a pointer and obliterate its possibility by eliminating its thrust, what have you accomplished? If you eliminate its thrust towards deeper understanding, you eliminate the revelation waiting just below the surface which now doesn't show itself. Awakening is seeing who you really are and having your ego identification release itself. You have to see who you really are before any of that can happen.

Where do I see this happening in the spiritual journey? As I often say, there is one basic to the path of wisdom. That is to see that you are the subject of misidentification. You believe you are the story identity or ego identity. You live "as if" it were true. That means all of the pointers tend to point you in the direction of pure consciousness or awareness because of your leaning already in the direction of the ego. You need to rebalance. Does this mean that the story or ego self will no longer arise or appear? No, it does not. But it is likely that any acknowledgement of that ego self isn't necessary in the pointer. Did the bicycle master run along and yell "Lean to the left, lean to the left, but don't forget that there is a right!" No, he didn't. He didn't need to as the student was already leaning too far to the right.

And please, if you have read this far, I know that you have that seekers pit in your stomach and you know intuitively there is something you must seek. So put your ego self on the shelf and use pointers to balance your bike.

Is This Kindergarten?

I must warn you that to many this story journey will appear to be childlike and beneath your obvious capabilities. You will be judged, more often by yourself than others, for your descent into the simple. Why is that? Let's talk about another assumption. Our intellectual heritage has chosen to worship luminaries who have looked at experience and described in elegant ways what they have seen as they gazed through the window. And in our admiration of that impressive extraction, we have conflated what their position really is. We think that what they say has something to do with experience itself. And perhaps it does if used as a pointer to a deepening journey. Most often, this is not the case. Rather, story and experience itself have been denigrated in favor of intellectual output.

But what is the difference I am teasing out here? Why is it important to see that looking through the window to an activity below is not being in the activity itself? It's because in our intellectual assent we have conflated the two. Now we unbraid the conflation. I assure you that if you looked out of the window onto a children's playground and extracted some brilliant concept, the broadcasting of that observation back into the playground would be hardly seen as wisdom. Children immediately know the difference between narrative and tangible being. For the children would immediately recognize that this insight has little to do with building castles in the sandbox. But generally, as humans we have ignored this distinction. And we have stood gluttonously waiting for the next brilliant concept to burst into our life. And while it is easy to see that this is simply is not possible, we ignore that and greedily ask for more. Somewhere inside we assume if we can become smart enough to look from inside the window that others will think that we are feeding them. Pointers seek to disassemble this assumption. Utilizing pointers is the rigorous and incessant stance that assumptive states must be penetrated and dissolved. And it is through the ongoing recognition and awareness that arises through you that brings the possibility of seeking and understanding the "Who am I?"

The history of such seeking has taken on many forms throughout time. Buddha, Socrates, Lao Tsu, and Christ were early adopters of a transformational lifestyle. They themselves were seekers and in their own journey held the doorway open for hordes of future seekers. In recent times we have had brilliant masters in various cultures that have furthered the reach of mysticism. Their names are too many to mention. But in all of this there has yet to arise a path that would be deemed germane to Western and American cultural roots. Certainly, it should be clear to most from the West that story is our birthright. Joseph Campbell was one of the first who began the inquiry into the nature of story, specifically myth. He often translated the stories and concepts of other cultures into versions that we could readily digest. And in a certain way it is on his shoulders that we stand with the intent to turn what many assume are his conclusions into pointers that will invite them into experience itself.

You Can't Experience It From Here, But Where?

This inquiry is not one of maps and concepts, rather one of the embracing of life. Its authenticity is not of the mind, but rather of the grittiness of life itself. One of my favorite places in the world is the cove on the island of Catalina, off the southern coast of California. The water can be as deep as 100 feet and is crystal clear. For viewing the flora and fauna, a glass bottom boat is a wonderful thing. But while it is a beautiful view, it is not an experience in the ocean. The distinction between the intellectual and the experiential is captured in this metaphor.

In the intellectual conversation, I often feel as though I am taking a trip in a glass bottom boat, peering into perfect clarity as we pass over the ocean floor below. As I do so, I see the beauty of the colors of the fish and other wildlife. Like on any such tour we have a guide locating these beautiful colors in a mental map so we can understand the ecosystem that we are traveling over. During such tours, I cannot shake the feeling that my guides, while robust in their knowledge of what I am seeing, have never themselves wallowed in the waters of the ocean below. They stand observing what lies in the depths. And in their very stance, they seem to sap the vibrant aliveness of the colorful field of watery profundity by describing and judging but never relinquishing the distance they seem to love.

It is a subtle violence that their crystalized grip on boundaries demands as they push a definitional frame into water, which pays no attention to their efforts. Much like attempting to categorize consciousness itself, the water pays no heed to their convenient cookie cutter version of all that is. Often you can hear the anguish in their own voice as they recognize the lost possibility of what they see as undeniable brilliance. Such brilliance is unable to land and make a difference, but we pretend it can.

Much like speaking to someone who isn't fluent in our own language, we speak louder and emphasize each word as though that were a substitute for fluency. This renewed and heightened attack that attempts to convince the touristic minions, with heightened faux confidence, that the guide knows what the water under the glass really feels like. Unfortunately, much like the emperor's new clothes, this approach depends on selling the idea that something is happening when it really is not.

So how revolutionary would it be to suggest that such brilliance could be utilized in an entirely different way? What if, instead of looking at the game of transformation from the press box and then trying to run on the field, we recognize that we are players? Rather than commentators, we would have experience as the Ground Zero to inform our colorful map. This approach would simply have the players root into the game itself and let the observers report what they see. The map would have to take on an entirely different function in this newly contextualized approach, for it would be informed from the field rather than the press box. Vibrantly alive instead of distant, observing, and remote. Change would not be taken on from the perch of a distant reflection of what is. Is it possible that a powerful experiential approach is available instead? And can it be rooted in the seekers path, which extends beyond the egos and their groupings that it identifies and colors? Is it possible that that the delivery of the map requires stance in a place beyond ego?

I am asserting exactly that.

chapter four

———•◦ ⚬⚬⚬ ◦•———

Life moves Through me

ONE OF MY FAVORITE stories as pointers toward awakening involves Osho. Its purpose? To dissolve, even jar, your story, your identity of separation. Ego, or the story identity, is exclusively a figment of separation. Ask yourself, is the way things happen really the way they happen? Could it all be another way? Are you willing to let what is unconscious in you dissolve and be replaced by another possibility? Let's tackle the very way you assume you move through life. But who moves through what or what moves through whom?

Ultimately, the moment of awakening, momentary or permanent, is a function of a perceptive shift. The story identity, or ego, has taken ownership of the position of your perceiving within your intellect. That intellectual frame is conflated with tangible perception to such a point that cognition itself locates perception in the ego. This state is often referred to as the split mind. The ego mind is busy usurping consciousness to form one perceptive slant. And there is consciousness, doing the perceiving, yet in an unrecognized way as though it were never there.

Okay back to the story. This one involves Osho's frequent and surprise attempts to jolt the seekers around him into another way of experiencing so-called reality. This story involves his ashram in Pune, India, which stood in the middle of a city block some five hundred yards from the corner. At that corner stood The German Bakery (its real name) which was the tea and pastry stop for hundreds of his followers. It was our daily stop on the way to sit with Osho. As we would turn the corner from the bakery, the buildings of the commune would slowly come into sight. This was almost a ritual and that sight was a welcome anchor in the density and sometimes rattling chaos of India itself.

One night, Osho hatched a colossal surprise. He had an army of artists paint the walls of the ashram totally black. What had formerly been a familiar and colorful welcome weas now transformed into an entirely different almost shocking experience. As his followers rounded the corner that day, they immediately felt that something was seriously amiss. As they neared the entrance of the ashram that feeling would have only grown. Many thought they were lost. And in a way, they were. This paint job was for them, a tangible pointer whose job was to jar the story frames that his seekers always held. Things are not always what they seem. Drop the assumptions about what is…because it isn't always the case. So, paint your world black a bit!

But before you do, let's make sure you understand the story of painting black. The way our ego operates is to establish both itself and its environment as an intellectual concept. Remember, intellect is the home of separation. It is there that particulars can both be defined and held separately, but related. You see? In the mind, the king's seat of the ego, is where your reality is held. Does it change? It sure does, but typically those changes are simply updates to the current version. The pointer approach is intended to dissolve your holdings in separation in the hope that the floor of your story will collapse, and you find yourself in being or presence.

What does this have to do with black buildings? Your ego holds the world it lives within as an assumption that it will continue and always be the same. By sudden change in the world around you, you can dissolve and even shatter your ego frame. In the gap between the old holding and the new, all that is available is you, as presence. No intellect, no concept, no frame, no separation. The beauty of the story of the black walls is that it is tangible. The change induced by Osho was not one of intellect. By changing the tangible world, he could help change his followers' experience that ego does not just play in the pond of their minds, but it does indeed reach into the objects of hard existence. Is there anywhere that you are not in the mind? Yes, there is. In presence or consciousness.

Spiritual teachers are always shooting for the gap. What gap? The one I have described here, where the mind is caught unawares and collapses into being. There is a Buddha story about desire. Buddha asserted the only time an ego feels at peace is in a gap moment. Which moment is that? The moment in which a desire has been fulfilled and before the next desire has taken its place. The ego uses desire the same way it holds on to its surroundings such as buildings. Painting the walls black is an inducement to fall into the gap. Of course, we are never taught such things in the egoic world. Why should we be? In what way does dissolving the hold of the ego serve a world directed by the ego? So, this is your chance to know how to look somewhere different. The master will not spend a lot of time discussing the theory and notion of water, but rather will listen for the splash.

The one thing we all know is that there is a sense of existence. It can be felt in every moment. If you think about where you are in life at any age you know that there is something exactly the same now as has always been. When you were 5 years old you were in every moment in exactly the way you are now. Yes, your story has changed but there is a consistent, immutable you that is always in every moment. But wait, we always speak and assume that there is an entity called me that is moving through every moment as an independent traveler. Even I talk incessantly about the spiritual journey of the seeker as though that autonomous identification is moving through the rest of life itself. I do that so folks will understand my communication even though there is that assumption wrapped within.

So, we now know two things. You are the presence or sense of what is present from the moment you could perceive and remember. And all of the appearances, including your body and mind, happened and continue to happen in the presence of that presence. We then take that happening and create a story of an independent mover called Alan or some such and act "as if" that entity is making a journey. But here is what is seemingly really happening. You are always present to whatever appears to you including what you think is yourself. There literally is no "you" moving through life. Life itself is moving through you and you are both everlasting and always the same.

So, what do you do with this seemingly small difference? Begin to notice that the entirety of life is projected into your awareness anytime you are perceiving. Note that your perceiving has no beginning or ending. I am certain that you, like me, have not noticed a beginning to your awareness ever. What is that perceiving? It is who you really are. Can you see that in order to have a "you" that is walking through life that you have to make it up? In a story? But what is it really like when you do not make up that story and pretend that is what is happening? Well hallelujah! It turns out that you are infinite in time with no beginning and no end, and everything moves through you. You thought when you would hear such spiritual nuggets that some stuffed shirt of an intellectual was writing about the ethereal. Nope. You can sit your own little fanny down in a chair and experience it right now.

Ramesh once said, *"The one must awaken who was never asleep, and the one must sleep who was never awake"*. In other words, the one who through which the whole world moves must be recognized and perceived as operable and the story identity, which has been awake, can relax and even slumber. In other words, the fanny sitting part is the opportunity to experience a perceptual shift.

Now, you will notice that I use some of these spiritual nuggets. But what matters is reducing such comments into tangibility. What is that? It is making it simple and right now. It has to be felt. This pointer is just that. Does life move through you or do you move through it? Why does everyone describe it exactly backwards? If you believe you are a separate autonomous author of your own journey, then we should be able to find that entity travelling though his or her adventures. But as you sit there is not any such thing. Why do we do this? It is the story we have been handed. But we know, as my Grandpa Ed would have said, that there is something else going on out there. Yep. It turns out life moves through you. And you are just the watching perceiver. Oh yeah, they hung a body off of the perceiving as you might have noticed.

The well-known saint Nisargadatta said the following, *"A jeweler who wants to re-fashion an ornament first melts it down to shapeless gold. Similarly, one must return to one's original state before a new name and form can emerge. Death is essential for renewal."* The original state that is referenced by Nisargadatta is the state of formless awareness itself. It is the only state. It is actually who you are…and everyone else for that matter. However, it is one thing to say it and another entirely to arrive and recognize the tangible presence of the unformed. The death of your story opens up the gap into which tangibility lives.

The seekers' journey is exactly as Nisargadatta describes it. It is a return to the original and authentic. The new name and form, or as I call it the new story, is actually the original myth story within each of us that is waiting to be ignited. It isn't as if that story has not tried to emerge, but most of us mistakenly believe that the 'woulds', 'coulds' and 'shoulds' pounded into our cognition by the machinery of society, culture and religion is actually who we are. What that is, is the original myth story dissembled and reconstructed in a mental map that attempts to stand in for consciousness itself. When the descent into consciousness occurs, or as Nisargadatta calls it the return to one's original state, the possibility that the original myth will emerge untainted is in play. This is not a perception from the mind that assumes separate egos as its cover fee. Rather it is consciousness itself with no intellectual or conceptual bounds until cognition occurs and produces the story.

And now you know that you can both recognize and be in the place of pure consciousness itself. It is that felt sense of "me" that is there for everything that has ever appeared in your life. You have just given that appearance a story and mistakenly identified with it. Now the process is to reclaim the consciousness that is at the bottom of all of this as your original state. This is also called the "I Am" in spiritual literature including my writings. Nisargadatta said that his guru told him to simply sit or rest in the "I Am" and that was the only thing he needed to do. And that he did until his sense of perception shifted and he was awakened. As a last word, I hope you can see how simple and direct this all is. In the spiritual world we have all sorts of terms and phrases that seem impenetrable. Forget those. You know the sense of your own existence. Go be there. How simple is that?

chapter five

The Illusion
of Destination

ILLUSION AND HISTORY

WHY IS AN ILLUSION useful for the purposes of awakening? Many times, we speak of illusion as something so disconnected from any perception we have ever had, that it is not even congruent to perception at all. That is to say, it is imaginary or made up. When we speak of illusion, the imaginings of good psychedelics or comic book happenings are not what we are after. Illusion in spiritual parlance is the notion that we have constructed and embedded a plot in the story that we live moment to moment, that simply is not the case.

Take a look at the two pointers you have just read. In *Life Moves through Me* we dissolve the notion that there is some separate "you" moving through a separate terrain called life or some such. How do we do that? We ask you to locate your very experience and notice that all happenings really travel through you and your perception. It is easy to do and by so doing we now can dissolve an old story and create a new one. We call this new one a living understanding. In the second pointer, *Lean to the Left*, we show how we lift our story from a happening, but many times do not look carefully at what the point of the exercise really is. The bicycle master knows balance is fundamental to becoming a bicycle phenom. When we see his coaching we instead assume "lean to the left" is the secret. Your entire life story is a function of these two activities. First the assumption that we are something separate, and then the continual proclivity to extract the wrong notion from what we perceive. Both of these are story building deviations. We then are left with a story that makes us intuitively sense that something is wrong. At the bottom of it all you are consciousness itself, and the remains of that knowing gnaws at the intuitive.

This type of illusion, the story deviation type, is standard in the history of humanity. Humanity has lived in a world where the innocence and naivete of children makes available the onboarding of a story that serves separate interests of human systems. About now you must be wondering "when will he get to the pointer?" I will, but first see that you likely have innocently locked in a version of life that is agreed upon by the masses, and you are suspecting something is amiss. Now see that you are in the grand tradition of suspicious folks looking out on life and attempting to eliminate the illusions that must be the source of this intuitive discomfort. Here is a story from a suspicious life spectator of 2500 years ago.

THE CAVE REDUX

"I was identified with something that
was just a shadow, a projection.
It wasn't real. But that's all I knew so I assumed
it was all there was."

CHRISTO

Some 2500 years ago, humanity was gifted with a story called the Allegory of the Cave. It is often credited to Plato, but Plato, himself cites Socrates as the teller of the tale. No one knows for certain who authored it, but it has been told and retold over the years, by countless philosophers and storytellers. Yet, most of the time the story is shared from a decidedly intellectual orientation. Ultimately, though, the Allegory is a seekers' story seemingly intended on cracking the very code upon which intellect itself stands. That dissolution is exactly the stuff of the seekers' journey. It begs the question, "What was it like to experience the cave from the inside out?"

Guess what? It turns out that the fellow from the cave that was named Christo, a good Greek name, who has his story to tell.

It has been many years since I left the cave. Yet, it is only now that I can tell you the story of my internment. I call it such only now, for when I was taken there as a child, I was told that I was being sent as the fulfillment of my life's purpose. This was where everyone went. Those around me would say "Christo, this is the moment for which you have been created. You will now get to see the world in the way it was meant to be seen." Do I remember my days before the cave? Hardly.

But I do remember I awoke one morning in almost total darkness, in a space that felt warm. A fire seemed to hover nearby. My arms, body, and head were firmly fixed so that I could look in only one direction. I gazed ahead at a large rock wall. I knew there were others around me, but I could only feel them nearby and hear their grunts and bodily noises. On the wall I could see vague shapes move across like shadows and I could hear various sound effects and an occasional narrator who would speak about the shapes that fleeted by. This must be what life is truly all about, I thought.

I would go to sleep and then, always, awaken to the same experience—over and over and over. I had no sense of being imprisoned or constrained, even though as I look back now, I understand that was the actual case. Life, as I could tell it, had a story and purpose based on the meaning of the enigmatic projection on the wall. These images of life flickered and danced, and it was only later I understood them to be simply shadows, projected from the fire behind by which puppeteers of sorts made their projections known. I thought they were real. They were real, in a sense, as they were all I knew. That was my story.

One moment, I was seemingly freed, although again I didn't know I wasn't free already. As I stood up, I turned back and gazed at the light of the bright fire. It immediately blinded me. I felt such pain but gradually my vision began to accustom itself and I could see men and women carrying objects across a rock shelf in front of the fire. So, this is what created what was almost my whole life's point of view! I was shocked. Puppeteers were moving around props that made shadows that I took as real. The objects were all a mirage, an illusion.

At the time I am sure I didn't know the difference between an object and a shadow. So, it might be better said that I saw shadows in the form of humans moving objects which also would have been but shadows to me. If it seems confusing in the telling I can only tell you that it was infinitely more so to experience it. Of course, I had no reference point to even attempt to understand who these shadow people were. It took me a fair amount of time to even absorb what real objects were all about. I was overwhelmed and it was almost too much to bear to have my known existence uprooted with such immediacy.

I so desperately wanted my life back. I did not want to feel the enormous confusion of recognizing that my reality wasn't what I had held that it was. Pain and confusion ensued.

At some point, I was then dragged out of the mouth of the cave. Both the bright sunlight and the steepness of the path were almost unbearable. At first, all I could see were shadows. Eventually I could make out reflections, if there was a small body of water or the shiny veneer of a leaf nearby. In time, I could see all of life as it was intended to be. The shadows disappeared and I saw anew.

It was then that I began to see and feel the difference between my cave life and this new world. It was a great awakening. I recognized that I had indeed been imprisoned. I realized this life was infinitely better than inside the cave. What do I mean by better? I was able to understand that my cave life had been produced for me. I now know that this production was not particularly mean spirited on behalf of those that seemed to want me to see the world in a certain way. But no matter, I could now see that there was a huge difference between the produced version of life and one that seemed original and intrinsic to my very humanity. I was no longer taking illusions for 'the real thing.'

I felt that I should return and let my fellow cave dwellers know of this new possibility. How could I leave them behind? When I re-entered the cave, I was again blinded, but this time, by the lack of light. When my sight returned, I could see my tied and bound previous comrades seemed terrified of my return. I could only assume that my temporary reaction of blindness upon reentering signaled that it was dangerous to leave the cave. I attempted to extol them with the amazing possibilities outside. But to my surprise, my former friends turned on me. I was now a threat and they wanted no part of anything I might want to tell them that contradicted the story they had been living.

Seekers over the millenniums have all played the part of Christo. And all seekers are hoping for the "Welcome Home" that Christo so long ago shared with his fellow travelers. It starts with acceptance of the story we are given. Then something happens to lead us to suspect that story. Now, in our story above, Plato simply tells us to imagine that Christo has been freed from the cave. But we can expand on this by knowing that these seeking stories are plentiful in our intellectual pursuits and seep into our being, igniting a suspicion. I like to think that Christo was freed by his seeker's drive. And then depending on the strength of that niggling, a seeker like Christo is born.

Isn't it amazing that Plato, some 2500 years ago, could see the very foundation of the spiritual quest? Did Plato or Socrates arrive and awaken? Who knows? But they certainly could see the charade that humanity orchestrated for themselves, and they created a story to lead us into a new understanding. Stories like the cave appear throughout the history of mankind as we have it. Children's tales, myths, philosophy, parables and religious texts all contain stories with an eerily similar theme. What theme is that? What you see is not always what is really going on. If you look deeper, you will see something more, the basis of real life. This is the essence of the spiritual quest for presence which is that foundational life essence.

THE ILLUSION OF DESTINATION

This is a simple pointer. It, like *Life Moves Through Me*, asks you to notice what your experience is. Then it lets you see that you have lived life with a different version of that experience. It is a repeat of believing the map is the territory. When in doubt look at your experience.

Where does a destination lie? You and I know that we all live in a daily reality that says it lies within our experience. But does it? Have you ever noticed that in life, no matter what destination you arrive at, nothing ends? The destination is at hand and life blithely continues its march. What is our response to this obvious ongoing? We place another destination into play. Where do we place it? Well, manifestation itself is seemingly intent on ignoring any of the punctuation that we tenaciously grab onto for the entirety of our lives. So, the only other place we hold such endings or arrival points is in our story.

Our story is but the fleeting movement of shadows on a cave wall and yet we sense there is something beyond. A story is constructed of separate elements intellectually distilled. It is in our story that we have created the notion of an ego self. This ego self is separate from the components, all the separate stuff that we call our environment. We overlay, much like Christo, a story which intends to separatize and even bestow autonomy to what we have extracted from our perceptive input. It is only in this overlay that a destination can be found. Destination lives in your mind. See if you have accepted a notion of life which seemingly includes destinations when none can be found in the actual living of that life.

So, who are you? Are you a story with autonomous egos and destinations that live animated within? Do you believe the conflation of your presence and being, which never begins and never ends, with the punctuation and mathematics of intellect? Life moves through you and it has no truncations other than those you and I attempt to force on a seamless flow. The perception of this seamless flow, and that flow itself, is who you really are.

chapter six

---•◦ ❧◊❧ ◦•---

The Assumptive state

ONE OF THE FIRST doorways to awakening is the recognition that life is an assumptive state. It is a story that our insecure ego demands be real. What do I mean by that? Because humanity has neatly decided that it is constituted of individuals with separate operating systems, volition included, all of life is packaged accordingly. This is the base assumption of human living. But what happens when we attempt to penetrate that assumption? And further, what do we actually know and what can we potentially know, that can become the central focus of this inquiry?

Rather than bore you with a philosophical discussion on epistemology, I think we can all agree that we really don't know exactly what we are. Every branch of academic study, every culture, and groupings of any kind establish as a central tenant what can be known and what cannot. Of course, this is done in order to support the reason that the group exists in the first place. Religious groupings utilize theological definitions to claim what can be known. Linguistic cultures do exactly the same. But underneath all of these meaningless tautologies lies the unexamined concepts upon which all of these conclusions are founded. And the principal inquiry that drives all others is: What exactly are we? Is each body the defining territory for what constitutes a separate individual? Or is each body connected in some way to the environment in which it lives?

This would mean that the boundaries of that individual extend somewhat beyond the body itself. What about a newborn baby? Most experts take the position that an infant has no sense of a boundary between himself and his mother. If this is true, is that boundary-less state more natural than the separation in which that child will ultimately live? The answer is we really do not know. But in order to live, the human intellect demands that it feels some level of surety to make its way. This sense of surety, based on an intellectual definition or concept, becomes a way of living. We live as though our claims are true. That is the assumptive state. It has a warp and woof. It is an ethos. I call it a state. And even our cognition intakes those data points, like masons use bricks, to contemporaneously keep our assumptive house feeling the way our concepts demand. We live in a construction. We all live a life "As If" the story we use to describe our living is the real deal. Wow!

KNOWING OR NOT

We could fill many volumes highlighting the things that we really don't know, that we assume are the case, in order to live our daily life. We could point to the fact that the assumptions we live within create all of the conflict in the world as we know it. For what is conflict? It is a disagreement of held assumptions. One government demands that their assumptive definitions are truer or more real than that of another. The same applies to religions and groupings of any kind. Further, in order to stand in such a holding, it is necessary that one ignore the fact that these assumed definitions are unfinished and clearly unsubstantiated. Separation coupled with confidence requires ignoring the obvious fact that one does not really know. And that 'not knowing' lingers under the surface of your outer construction beaming its understanding into your being. It makes you feel that something is just not right. You feel inauthentic. And then you think more intellectual construction is necessary. Why? Because we assume answers to all unsettledness can be found in intellectual construction. Now, there is one thing that we do know. We know that we exist. I would say that anything beyond that is an interpretation.

Multiply by Zero

One of my favorite pointers is from our early years in mathematics. I know. You have to be asking yourself "Who is this dude who now is using mathematics as a pointer?" But here we go. If you take a whole number and multiply it by another whole number, you will get a numerical result. In other words, a result will happen except for in a very particular case. What is that case? Mathematics, in order to work, needs a symbol that has no value. It turns out that having no value renders everything that is touched by that "no value" results in more no value. That symbol is the zero. It is my favorite thing in math. When you include a zero in a multiplication string of any size, the result immediately becomes zero. Wow.

The spiritual path is just like that. There is a zero in our midst that once introduced reduces all of our knowing to zero. We always assume in any discussion of humanity that we are composed of a group of individual entities. There is me and there is you. Once we have that established, we continue merrily along our way constructing all knowledge base on that assumption. But what would happen to all of that constructed knowledge if we perceived that the boundaries that make one of us "you" and the other "me" really did not exist? What if we could see that these delineations are there simply to create a narrative "as if" such were the case. It would be akin to finding the spiritual zero. That perception shifts the entire body of knowledge that humanity claims as its property.

All we know is that we experience a sense of existence. The rest is interpretation. What do we get to argue about now? You see why I say that? The interpretations ignore that there may be a spiritual zero underpinning them. Even ignored, the best we can say about any story we construct is that is has to be at most an interpretation. How could it be otherwise if a zero is at play and we pretend our story life does not include any? We can't call our possibly fictitious creations facts, could we?

Consciousness is Limited

At the root of consciousness lies desire, the urge to experience. So, consciousness itself plays into this very format. Consciousness is the enlivening element or energetic juice that makes all alive. It is what makes life a flow rather than a bunch of pieces. It has the malleability to organize around any system of belief. And in so doing it allows its participants to believe that their assumed definitions are in fact real. How does it do this? Simple. If the ground of knowing is rooted by felt experience, then consciousness is happy to deliver exactly that feeling. Thus, our assumptions become solidified in the felt experience of our own daily activity.

This tethering of our ego assumptions to the enlivening element of consciousness itself is called identification. The process of identification seduces the assumptive individual into the thinking that they are in fact what they have assumed themselves to be. And further, for many this sense of surety is so strong that further inquiry simply is not necessary. It is likely you aren't one of these simply by the fact that you are hearing this. I often call identification the glue that must dissolve in transformation. Many think the ego itself is annihilated in awakening. Nope. It is just the glue of identification that dissolves, leaving the ego as the navigator rather than the driver. So no, consciousness is not the good nor is it the bad guy. It delivers what the actors in its container have dreamed up.

We live in a world of technology, so let's think of it in that way. We have electricity which powers most all of our technological objects. Phones must be charged, and computers plugged in. Consciousness plays the role of electricity. Does electricity care what it is hooked up to? No, it sure doesn't. Consciousness, the electricity of life, doesn't either. It is simply a driver to whatever it is connected. Your body, and all objects in the perceptive world, are simply devices. Some devices run by themselves like can openers and vacuum cleaners. But the more sophisticated devices such as computers require software. Those devices need the capability to hold and execute on the software they hold.

It turns out that human body-minds are like those more sophisticated devices. In this case, our intellect is the capability to operate, and story is the software that runs our computer being. That is why I call our living an assumptive state. Once the software of story is in place, all of our activity runs on our story software. See, it is assumptive. Later I will dive into how behavior becomes automatic, but for now seeing our behavior as an unseen set of directions driven by a story works well enough. If you think about it, you must tell a story to the software developer to get the computer output result you have in mind. In our case, we have the entirety of humanity crashing down on us only too happy to share their story about who we are, insisting we include it in our software.

But there is a feature in being human that lies outside this metaphorical imagining. We are equipped to be the perceiver of awareness and consciousness itself. That gets derailed by the story of separation which we hold and on which we operate. But we know in a non-intellectual place called intuition that our software is not the version that allows our perfect sense of being human to express itself. That niggling or incongruity creates discomfort internally and can create a seeker.

The Seeking Transmission

Beyond consciousness, in awareness itself, lies the apperception that dissolves the definitional perceptions that seemingly make up the world, as we know it. And when this door is opened, the channel between awareness and consciousness, the energy of seekership bursts through. The intuition that something more must be discovered cannot be denied and a seeker is born.

Of course, most every seeker believes that a new set of definitions is exactly what they now are undertaking. But in reality, what is being asked is that consciousness itself becomes an open possibility to whatever arises in any given moment. And this open possibility requires no definitions whatsoever. For this reason, the seeker is driven to move out of the assumption that a discovery of intellectual definitions is connected in any way to awakening. Rather, it has to be seen that awakening is a phenomenal shift in being and its subsequent felt experience within being. As a result, intellectual concepts or definitions can only serve as pointers to the possibility of that phenomenal shift. And in order for these pointers to move the 'seeker in consciousness' into being, the standard death grip of identification must not be in play.

How do we do this? By understanding that all life lived

in apparent separation is an assumptive state. This experiential and phenomenal holding will allow consciousness to express itself in a different way than heretofore experienced. That different way will be naturally closer to awakening. As we have discovered, consciousness is engaged in revealing itself to itself in duality. This revealing can be pointed to intellectually, but never held within the conceptual map. But be aware that your likely held assumption is that it can live in the map of the mind. Identification is the conflation of your story identity with experience itself. Most folks cannot see that this is how they really live.

YOUR THEORY OF EVERYTHING

I am often asked "Did you look for new information rather than pointers in your early seeking?" I sure did! I cannot help but remember my early days in the ashram in Pune, India. Every night, at 6 o'clock, the entire community would gather in white robes to listen to a discourse of an hour or two from Osho. In those days I was convinced that if I could absorb the obviously superior information that was being delivered in his discourses and place them properly in Alan's "Theory of Everything" that enlightenment was eminent. Of course, the inevitable would occur. I would rush home from a discourse full of a variety of things that needed to have footing in how I thought the world was constructed. I would normally spend the majority of the evening and into the early morning reformulating my entire worldview. And then the next evening I would attend the next discourse. And guess what? I would now have a new group of concepts that needed to find their home in my theory, which unfailingly required that I adjust all the previous concepts that most likely had newly rooted.

This process went on for several months until it became obvious that nothing in my felt experience was affected by this exercise other than an ongoing lack of sleep! This experience morphed into this pointer: *The understanding of transformation is not an intellectual exercise.* You may note in yourself this very same assumption regarding intellect and, in fact, you may be attempting to locate the words of all the wise men in history into your own theory of everything. It is this very assumption that humanity at large makes and has libraries filled with the memorials to all sorts of egos arranged in a nice subject categorization. But has anyone ever questioned or proved that ego massaging is anything other than self-indulgence? This pointer is simply an invitation to see the insanity of this particular process and actually step into the phenomenality of arising consciousness. Of course, you are welcome to continue the approach much as I did. If it indeed changes the experience of consciousness feel free to let me know.

WE LIVE "AS IF"

We all live in an assumptive state. Our life is a function of 'As If'. That is to say, we live as if we understand how consciousness actually operates. But who instructed us that this understanding is even part of what we are designed to do? This pointer is an invitation to unburden yourself with the assumption that you have the intellect to hold something called the theory of everything. It is an invitation to stand in every moment and see the nature of 'As If' such that the deeper expression of consciousness can be recognized.

There was a saintly man, a Sufi master. He lived in a small village in the typical hut. One day a neighboring young woman discovered she was pregnant. This news was followed by the inevitable, the birth of her daughter. Everyone in the village wanted to know the identity of the father. The woman, being single, did not want to reveal her lover's name so instead, she named the Sufi master as the father. The community demanded that this Sufi bring up his new daughter. When they all arrived to see to her, he said simply "All right, leave my child". Over the next few years, he tended to the child. But as you might imagine, things changed and the young mother married her lover, recanted her story, and confessed that the Sufi was not the father of the child. The village went to the Sufi and apologized, "We are very sorry we made this mistake. Would you please give the child back?" He said simply "All right, take my child."

The first step in the spiritual journey is following in the steps of the Sufi master. It is the recognition that the story you are living is simply the one that works that day. That story is not you and believing it to be so is the root of your internal misery. If the village thinks you are the father, then so be it. If the village wants their daughter back, then so be it. Neither of these stories is who you are anyway unless you assume, and a willing consciousness follows along.

THE HICK VERSION

When I write in the terms I have used thus far, a lot of folks typically complain that I am hard to read. This always reminds me of a David Allan Coe country song. At first it is believed to be the perfect country song. But wait, not so fast. It turns out that a final verse needs to be added to include such things as Momma, a train, getting drunk and prison. And with these final hick additions the perfect country song is born.

Here is the hick version of knowing it all. Either we know stuff, or we don't. Turns out that we aren't satisfied with that. There is so much stuff we do not know that we just make shit up. Then to feel good inside we pretend it is real. That is called belief. Imagine you walk into a barn and there you see a snake. You pull out the rake and beat it to a pulp. And when you are done you notice that it is not a snake at all but a piece of rope. Before you figured that out, you were acting 'as if' it was a snake.

Well, in our story we have made an entire life up much like that snake. And we spend all our time beating the hell out of life like it was a snake. We have wars, arrest folks and do downright mean crap because we think we know. But we don't. That is all I am saying here. To start getting rid of that feeling that "something is wrong here" you just have to see that you don't know as much as you think. In fact, you don't know much at all! Bottom line is that if we are naturally meant to feel at home by being some other way, we have got to let the current version go. Make sense? If you want to park a car in the garage you might need to take the one that is already in there now out. The rest of the stuff about duality and consciousness are just a fancy ass way of talking about what we see and what is the juice that makes us alive. The assumptive state is just the shit an entire humanity has agreed on and given to you. And we all act 'as if' that were true. Ta da.

chapter seven

———•◦ ⚙ ◦•———

what wants to happen

A S A CHILD IN church, I used to hear the tale about
Jonah and the whale. It was one of my favorites. Jonah was this fellow who hung around with God some 800
years BC. In fact, God decided that Jonah should handle a
few housekeeping chores for him. It seems that there was
this city called Nineveh and God simply did not like the
way they handled things there. So, God said to himself
"Let's give these Nineveh folks 40 days to straighten up or
I will simply destroy the place." Then he decided he would
have his boy, Jonah, roll into Nineveh and deliver the news.

Perfect plan. Well, except for the part where Jonah
headed out on a ship to some other city so he would not
have to go to Nineveh. And God said to himself "Really?" So, God whipped up a really big storm that threatened
to sink Jonah's ship. The sailors on the ship could sense
that something was wrong, so they picked straws and Jonah got the short one. He obviously was the problem and
the sailors simply threw him into the ocean and the storm
passed. Good news for the sailors. However, Jonah was

now in the ocean and God had his other buddy, the whale, simply swallow him for a few days. And, in due, God had the whale simply burp Jonah onto the nearest beach to Nineveh. By then Jonah was willing to do whatever as it is really crowded and cramped in a whale's belly. Well, what does this have to do with today?

In my own life I left the corporate world at the age of 37 to spend some years in the ashrams of India seeking out enlightened sages to sort out my own life. It was an incredible immersion into wisdom and consciousness. Upon my return to the West, I decided that I would never enter the corporate world again. I would find something new. However, the world would not cooperate. No matter how hard I tried, the only thing that came my way was, you guessed it, corporate work. It turns out that I was a corporate kind of guy who is built to engage in the wisdom traditions of leadership and presence in the corporate landscape. But I had decided otherwise. And much like Jonah, the whale kept swallowing me and burping me up on the corporate beach. In fact, I ate sand so often that I finally, like Jonah, gave in and began to accept the natural story that belongs to only me.

It was in this experience that I began to understand that each human being is a story that is already formed and simply waiting for ignition. Many do not even see this and pursue some other story as handed to them by society and the like. But, if they look closely, they will find where the whale has swallowed them and which beach he wants to burp them onto. I saw that if one could find their original story, they could rent a nice Jeep and take a picnic basket to the beach rather than my approach, which left me standing, dripping in some whale's digestive juices.

We just covered a chapter called the assumptive state. That is your activity as lived out of inherited story programming. Now this usually creates an experience of ongoing turbulence in life, as you are overriding another possibility. That possibility is life lived as your original story (not the mutated, inherited one), which is always available if uncovered. This is a life of perfect peace as there is no dissonance between two competing stories with one overriding the other. In my Jonah story you can see that, if given a chance, you can take the Jeep to the beach, no turbulence there, as opposed to fighting for air in a whale's belly.

Is This the Same as "What Wants to Happen?"

Yep. Here is a pointer. *"What wants to happen?"* Why is that important? Because your original story wants to happen. And there is one choice we all have, which is to let it happen or fight it internally and watch it happen anyway. In this pointer we have a whale, and damn they are big, that makes what wants to happen, happen. Our recognition of exactly that movement removes the turbulence of the mind that otherwise might think that it is in charge.

Concepts are intellectual constructions that demand that every individual story is equal or in some way the same. Concepts are rarely challenged as to their homogenous necessity. Further, they are migrated into the human mind as though they were experience itself. Conversely, story is an individual extraction from experience itself. Story is able to hold the sense of movement itself. It has tangibility, when properly delivered, that invites all to stand in an experience in the moment of telling. What we all see in front of us is an arising within and of consciousness. Pure awareness itself, not tinged in any way, emerges as cognized story. Story is the only container that is the conduit from nothingness to somethingness. Story holds both ends of the manifestation process.

WHAT'S ORIGINAL MYTH?

This brings us to Original Myth. What is that? Original Myth, in contemporary terms, could most likely be traced back to Joseph Campbell. He suggested that individuals and relationships hold, at their beginning or source, a rooted, authentic and original story. It is a one-of-a-kind thing. Over a lifetime, most individuals unwittingly forget that story and replace it with a society version of woulds, coulds, and shoulds. We lather over our original essential story with synthetic story plaster given to us by others. It must be obvious that giving up our *Original Myth Story* for any other replacement story robs us of our own most powerful possibility. It also places much of our experience in the throes of turbulence as we mentally buck the whales in our Jonah's tale.

One of the central tools in seeking can be the experience of finding one's original myth. Myth, in this case, is not something that is untrue, which is a common definition. But rather points to the essence of a human being as capsulated in a story. The Greek myths would be a good example of essences rendered into archetypal stories. The idea of an original myth is also nested in the East's notion of "I Am". "I Am" is the first defined essence that emerges from the undifferentiated consciousness that we individually are deemed to be. From the moment of the emergence of this "I Am", an arc of individual human experience, or tangible story, begins. We each have our own beach on which we are perfectly at home. Finding your original myth is simply tracking back to the original authenticity that you are. It is the simple finding of that story which holds the essence of your first emergence.

If we will simply remember back to the early years of childhood and the experience of reading fairytales, the sense of story becomes profoundly multidimensional. In these early years it was not uncommon to pull a fairytale from the shelf with the intent to live within the very covers of that book. As a child we could be the hero, the dragon, and any of the assorted sidekicks, of such tales. This experience was much more than the reading or even the telling of the story. In fact, it would be common to spend time exploring the energetic realms that small books thrust into the consciousness of a child. Really, it is the reverse. The consciousness of the child is the field of her original myth. The book has entered her field. And this original myth field can be explored, much like an enchanted land, by children and, you guessed it, adults. Only to get adults to visit we need to create big concepts like "Original Myth Process" so the adult can go with credibility a child would never need.

The point of the original myth process is to evoke the unique sense of a deep and profound field of consciousness, such that a seeker can find their way back to who they really are. That is to say that the unique snowflake of individuality can only be embedded in the story that its seeker can find. And they, and only they, are the ones who can find that field. When utilizing this process, it is important to understand that there is no time limit. Many people will take weeks, months, and even years descending on their own personal elevator to the basement where their original myth has always been housed. It is thus necessary to create a sense of relaxation combined with an expectation that the process will live itself. All individual personal effort is antithetical to this process.

Another important understanding of individual story is that the original myth lives in parts and pieces in subsequent stories in a personal lifetime. This means that when asked to find the original myth story, that another later and resonant story might draw the attention of the participant. This is a perfect result. The seeker should find the story in herself that has the strongest energetic. If this is not the original myth story, no problem. Over time it is not unusual that the first found story holds a piece of the energetic and will dissolve when a deeper version of the story makes itself known. Many people have been known to move through 10 or 12 stories before they feel that they have indeed arrived at the original myth story. But the key to all of this is to open the door to the journey rather than create individual effort to push to a right answer. There is no right answer. Whichever story is the strongest in any moment will be the story that allows the individual to stand in rooted authenticity, as authenticity is known in that moment.

The journey to the original myth is one that is never-ending. This process is simply the first stab at finding the unique proposition that each human "is". Therefore, it is necessary to know to stay open and aware of the deepening of this journey that will be happening within. Today's story may disappear into a deeper and more profound story that makes itself known in the future. Vigilance and awareness are the stalwarts that facilitate this ongoing journey.

Much like my own story of the Jonah-like adventure, finding one's original myth begins to reveal the arising elements of your story in a whole new way. You might see, much like I did, that my story was delivering me to places that were confusing yet immensely powerful. Over the years I have watched hundreds engage with this descent into themselves. And the presence of these folks has deepened and shown the path to presence and authentic living we all intuitively know are the environs of sages. You know it when you feel the power of presence of extraordinary leaders. When asked, they will likely tell you a story. What kind? Certainly, the kind with elements of *The Original Myth*.

Is There a Real-life Example
of This Pointer?

This pointer "*What Wants to Happen*" is the perfect companion to understanding that your original myth is that story which operates perfectly in synch with the movement of what wants to happen. So, let's spend a minute and delve a bit into the Original Myth process and why the road to awakening can be transited through that story.

I happened on this pointer-process I call *The Original Myth* when I was training corporate leaders to cultivate the magnetic presence that they sought. Yep, they were looking for the authentic version of themselves. This is the way in. Find a quiet place and take a half an hour or so without interruptions. Settle down. Breathe, relax, get comfortable. Now go back in your memory to some good things in your childhood. Think of some of the stories you loved back then. Remember how much you resonated with these stories. Or at least choose one that touched you deeply. You may have read books or listened to adults tell wonderful tales. You may have watched stories on television or in the movies. Your story can also be an experience you actually had that stuck with you, that made a deep "Aha" inside of you. Notice the sense of how real those stories felt to you. This sense of remembering and feeling what actually still is I call your meta-skill. You will use it as you continue the process.

Once you have established this child story sense, go back into your memory and even recite one of the stories out loud or quietly to yourself. This can make the experience feel more real. Now ask yourself: "What is the story from all of the stories that is most like me?" There are certain things that likely will appear in the stories that are most like you. Now, my story is experiential, as well as many told to me by my grandfather. This one really made me know something inside and out.

As a very young child, I was raised close to the ocean. My uncle and his friends routinely took me to the ocean and put me on every kind of board you can imagine. Surfboards, boogie boards and everything in between. I felt connected, in love, and exuberant even as a young child. It was my natural place. But then it happened, we moved. I ended up in a small village where agriculture, specifically oranges, were the main livelihood of our town. There was no ocean of any kind. I longed for my reunions with my beloved ocean and the boards that made me feel one with her.

Then, one day, I saw a head bobbing up and down in the distance coming towards me at an incredible speed. I looked down and saw what looked to be a surfboard on wheels. In that moment, my world exploded. A skateboard!!! You see, even as a small boy, I knew that a surfboard with wheels made the entire world an ocean. I had been released to my natural place of being in love with surfing the planet. My beloved ocean had heard the cries of a small boy and annexed the rest of the world so he could ride his board! To this day I recite that story to myself whenever I enter into a situation that calls for executive presence. I am known for sitting in the lobby, head down, lips moving before every big meeting. What am I doing?

Reciting my original myth story.

Back to the process. Once you have found that story, recite it to yourself. See if it doesn't almost speak itself right through you, the way your stories and experiences did when you were a child. Use the metaskill—feel the sense of what your stories were when you were a child, when they felt tangible and real. Once you have arrived at this story, create a video of yourself. Tell this story out loud. Shoot the video as many times as you wish, until you feel the story and you know it is you. This is an original myth story. You may discover new and different stories and world changing experiences that are even stronger from time to time. No worries. Go through the same process with them. You see, it is not in the descriptive bits of your story but the energy of the story that is actually you. Your stories hold the energy of you. Follow that energy and it will lead you to your strongest version of presence.

So now that I have told you one of my original myth stories, let's see if we can take you to the place where, like a child, you might have constructed your play fort and invited all your peeps in. Everyone knows that I love dogs. The rescues simply take my heart, and I am in service always to them. So, for you dog people here is one of my favorites I use to demonstrate the felt sense of depth in diving into story.

A farmer had some puppies he needed to sell. He painted a sign advertising the 4 pups and set about nailing it to a post on the edge of his yard. As he was driving the last nail into the post, he felt a tug on his overalls. He looked down into the eyes of a little boy.

"Mister," he said, "I want to buy one of your puppies."

"Well," said the farmer, as he rubbed the sweat off the back of his neck, "These puppies come from fine parents and cost a good deal of money."

The boy dropped his head for a moment. Then reaching deep into his pocket, he pulled out a handful of change and held it up to the farmer.

"I've got thirty-nine cents. Is that enough to take a look?"

"Sure," said the farmer. And with that he let out a whistle. "Here, Dolly!" he called.

Out from the doghouse and down the ramp ran Dolly followed by four little balls of fur. The little boy pressed his face against the chain link fence. His eyes danced with delight. As the dogs made their way to the fence, the little boy noticed something else stirring inside the doghouse.

Slowly another little ball appeared, this one noticeably smaller. Down the ramp it slid. Then, in a somewhat awkward manner, the little pup began hobbling toward the others, doing its best to catch up...

"I want that one," the little boy said, pointing to the runt.

The farmer knelt down at the boy's side and said, "Son, you don't want that puppy. He will never be able to run and play with you like these other dogs would."

With that the little boy stepped back from the fence, reached down, and began rolling up one leg of his trousers. In doing so he revealed a steel brace running down both sides of his leg attaching itself to a specially made shoe. Looking back up at the farmer, he said, "You see sir, I don't run too well myself, and he will need someone who understands."

With tears in his eyes, the farmer reached down and picked up the

little pup. Holding it carefully he handed it to the little boy.
*   "How much?" asked the little boy...*
*   "No charge," answered the farmer, "There's no charge for love."*

AUTHOR UNKNOWN

Are you crying right now? The words are looking a little blurry to me for sure. Now go into the feeling that you are having. Do you see any words or stories in there? Nope. What is happening is that consciousness is flowing feeling through you. If this story affects you greatly, then you know it is likely a piece of your own original myth. What is happening here? This story is a demonstration of how a little boy sees a dog who is, for all the world, just like him. In fact, he is so much so that he wants to keep him as part of his life. He and the dog are the same thing. We call that sameness love. Yes, the emotional energy is pulsing through you as you read it and that is because the move towards prior unity is evoked. It is quiet to be sure, but the emotion that consciousness generates through you as a pipeline is hard to contain. This is what to look for in your own early stories. What are the things that make you come alive when you re-enter that magic child's kingdom that is still living inside of you? And look at the lack of boundaries and intellectual dicta that this story holds. That sense is outside of intellect. It has nothing to say or if it does t's nonsense.

Now, you may notice that this exercise does not take you beyond yourself as an egoic entity. That is true. It was constructed to move executives to a place of more presence and authenticity on the way home, to awakening. That said, recognize that this place of authentic ego is on the way. I often comment that it is just one stop before. How does that work? Remember that the awakening movement is one of dealing with a mistaken identity. Its essence is a retracing to the essence that you are before you adopted the definition of society and lived it as though it were real. What is the recognition that reveals the last stop on the line? Glad you asked.

I often use the example of a cup. A cup? The first time I taught this pointer it hit me that a cup could be used as a prop. I promptly grabbed one off my desk and it happened to be a Starbucks cup. Yep, that's right. Now when I present this exercise, I hold up a cup for all to see. A cup is a cup is a cup. So, follow along as I attempt to do this in words. Imagine you are the cup. You are the container which holds all of the content that makes you, you. That should be easy to compare to an ego. Your ego is basically a self-contained object which holds what you are.

Now imagine that you, the cup, travel on a flat surface. When I demonstrate, I usually hold up a notepad or a large book and move the cup around on the platform. So, there you go, wandering about all the world as an independent container. Now stop and picture what I have said. There is a cup. That cup is on a board, notepad or other such plane. We believe we are independent wanderers in our own story. The cup represents you as a body mind or an independent container. The board or plane is the terrain upon which you travel or move around. It is your world, as it were. But is our natural story one of wandering as an independent object on a plane we call our environment?

Now, imagine that the reason you wander about in such a way is that you have been taught with woulds, coulds, or shoulds that your life can be nourishing while wandering. Then along comes some corporate consultant who tells you about authenticity. He tells you that you will feel more nourished and operate at your best when you are located, in fact glued, right on your perfect spot on the board. This is the spot of authenticity. Imagine now that you are the cup, perfectly glued on the board on your perfect spot, and you feel the vibrant connection to who you really are. Now, there is more to this dance. The something more is the piece that turns this exercise from one of leadership training to spiritual awakening. When you are glued to a spot egoically as a container you will simply be a more stable ego. So, what is next for those that wish to dive into the final act of seekership?

Here we go. You are not a cup at all! Your 'cupness' is simply a case of mistaken identity. Well then, what in the world are you? I teach that sitting permanently on your authentic space is a presence booster. But what if you lopped off the bottom of the cup and saw that what you really are is a conduit? There is no cup bottom between you and the terrain or board which is consciousness itself. All along you have been connected but couldn't see that because of the story you hold of being a cup. Your real perception is obfuscated by the story you live "as if" you were a cup. Knock off the bottom and replace the cup story with the conduit story. You, the cup, are there. Your world, the board, is still there. You used to think they were two things even if you thought they were interdependent. Now you can see that you and your world are one thing. See it as plainly as day and you have awakened. The road to the original myth as an ego is the same road of recovering your mistaken identity, minus one stop. This entire exercise of pointers, new stories and elements are all in the service of your awakening. But I assure you that you will know upon awakening that you have returned home to your original myth or original face or consciousness itself. Knock off the bottom of your cup. Got it?

You might think that all of this is esoteric or beyond the average bear. That is what I used to think, as well. But there I was, teaching corporate leaders who seemingly had no stake in spiritual outcomes. They cared about the bottom line and performance. But they also cared about presence. Each of them could tell you when they had been in the presence of great leadership. They could feel it and had connected that feeling to wisdom in leadership. That connection seems to be an intuitive one throughout all paths of endeavor. And here are some of their direct quotes. One fellow said, "My perceiving is no longer from what I have always thought was me." When I asked what he knew about presence now he replied, "It doesn't come from me, but it's bigger than me, yet comes through me". Another woman, the CEO of a large apparel brand, said "I know what I have always thought was me is clearly not me". Wow! These are corporate folks talking about something way bigger than stockholder concerns.

So, here I was in the middle of what we all had claimed was a spiritual wasteland listening to descriptions of personal experiences of having a spiritual presence. Often, I use the pointer that we are all included. You see, we have been taught that when we look out on manifestation, we actually exclude ourselves. But presence holds us inside that manifestation. When we are looking out, we actually are seeing from consciousness itself, even though we locate ourselves on the outside in our story and custom. This exercise bursts you through that supposed barrier.

I cherish the days that I sat with the "Father of Modern Management," Peter Drucker, on a sunlit patio inside the cozy Claremont Colleges, in Southern California. Peter was an amazing mentor before I went off on my trek to India. He shared with me his pet issue. He was a strong believer that private enterprise would have to become a main plank in our culture, and he was adamant that human concerns would have to replace shareholder concerns. While we have not seen that happen yet, our teaching within corporate organizations has broadened to include pointers toward presence and awakening. Matters of the heart, and beyond. Peter talked about how the essence of movement was not in the numbers, but in our hearts.

I vividly remember the last time I saw him. It was a week before I took off on my trek. "Alan," he said, "You are embarking into the land of the unseen. Gather all you can and bring it back. Figure out how to extend my paltry beginnings and continue mining the unseen so we can gift it to our beloved corporate world." Peter, unfortunately, had dementia in his last days and I never saw him again. But I will never forget his support in what at that time and in that context could look like a kooky dive into woo-woo land. He knew the unseen had gifts for all of us.

So, what wants to happen now? See yourself as part of the whole. The cup and the terrain are one and the same. All of these are pointers to an experience of who you really are. It happens anywhere, but always here and now. Wherever you spend your time is the terrain of awakening. And the beckoning of what wants to happen is always in the air.

For shits and grins here is a little ditty to remember this one. Someone will need to add the music!

Here's the deal.
You are the cup.
You are the cup on the platform.
The cup and the platform are one.
You are not the bottom of the cup. It's gone.
You are the conduit.
You are not the cup!!

chapter eight

———•◦ ⚬⚬⚬ ◦•———

faded versions

"Within the prison of your world appears a man who tells you that the world of painful contradictions, which you have created, is neither continuous nor permanent and is based on a misapprehension. He pleads with you to get out of it, by the same way by which you got into it. You got into it by forgetting what you are, and you will get out of it by knowing yourself as you are."

NISARGADATTA MAHARAJ

MUCH LIKE THE temblors of *Plato's Cave* and *The Emperor's New Clothes*, humanity has long harbored a sense that "something's not quite right here." And while this underground niggling bangs around within us, we somehow are still captured within our assumptive state. All pointers are designed to wake us up to that fierce construction we, as humans, have built to make sure the assumptive state continues to live itself out. Remember that this assumptive state is based on separation. Guess what else is based on that? The story of me or our ego. Our ego is the deepest story we have overlaying our original myth.

Faded Versions is another pointer in the family of notic-ings of how we have walled ourselves into our assumptive state, brick by brick. Faded versions are the weak, dis-tanced versions of intense story that we delude ourselves into thinking are superior, more scientific, elegant or even sophisticated. This paves the way for presence to be re-placed by conditioning. Deep rooting is replaced by short strokes of endless repetition.

Think for a minute about the notion of an original myth story. Joseph Campbell regarded the original myth story as one that was already there, ready to live itself, as a natural function of our composition in consciousness. This would be a natural emanation from the wholeness of who you are within the non-dual nature of awareness. But then the army of egos, called parents, teachers and authorities, implant the software of separation onto the in-nocent awaiting body-mind of a child. Voila! Now these well-meaning or not so well-meaning egos have given birth to a progeny of separation. A baby ego. In order to support such a baby, it is imperative that the world be an exercise in and construction of parts.

Now our stories, which are so close to pure awareness, must be upgraded into pieces and parts. The cult of sepa-ration worship is about to begin. If we can just use faded versions of story itself and organize them in a stilting, suf-focating, truncative cacophony, then the terrain for ego life is established. What in the world do I mean by this? Let's create stuff birthed by story but cut off at both ends. We will call these things concepts, formulas, theories and spreadsheets. We will even pretend they can stand alone with no regard for the underlying story itself. In fact, we will devise a process called education that purports to take one to dizzying heights of intellect by infusing it with worship of stuff with more parts and denigration for the stupidity of simplicity by claiming such are the domain of children and thus way below our status as fully realized adults! We have successfully turned the real world on its head.

Think a minute about your early life and the way you naturally learned. Language is the first thing you have to master in order to even participate in what we call humanity. How did that happen? I suspect the same way it happened to me. I have to surmise that my first language lesson happened one day when my Mom sat my diapered butt on the living room floor whilst doing some chore. Perhaps she was ironing in front of the TV. Or maybe baking. Where did my lesson start? It started with whatever words she used to deal with life as it was happening. My first word was cookie. I suspect that comes as no surprise to anyone that knows me. And my second word was cookie as well. What came next? Likely a lesson of diaper changing followed by explanations of soap operas, flowers, and other pertinent subjects. I, like all babies, was tossed into an ocean of words in an immersive experience. It was the only way to take a non-verbal child and verbalize him.

So, what normally happens when we learn our next language? Let me tell you my story. I speak a second language at a fairly developed level. That language is Spanish. Growing up in a village of orange growers with 60%

of the population of Mexican heritage, it should come as no surprise. But beyond the street words I, like many of my friends, did not learn Spanish until my late teens. My mother had converted to Mormonism when I was 7 years old and resultantly, I was pushed into that system. Of course, at the age of 19, I was expected to serve a two-year mission to some foreign country and mine was Peru.

In June of 1972 I flew to Utah and a couple of days later was domiciled for two months in the Language Training Mission. This was at Brigham Young University in Provo, Utah and we would spend the entire day, every day, learning Spanish in a classroom style. And we were expected to speak only 100% Spanish at all times. First, we learned verbs and objects. Then we learned tenses and sentence structure. We were expected to take this linear learning and migrate it into our spoken delivery. After these two months we were sent to our assigned country for the next 22 months.

I loved Spanish but I noticed something about the results of this particular learning experience. We all spoke with a fairly pronounced, non-Spanish accent. It was then that I began to notice that many folks who had a second language carry an accent, and some did not. Why? As I informally collected stories, I noticed that those who emerged from classroom learnings typically had more accented, less authentic language. My point here is that language best learned includes not just a 'blackboard', so to speak, but developing an ear that is sensitive to and creates less accented speech. Immersive rather than classroom learning seems to consistently reveal this significant improvement in speaking another language.

Why do the Dutch, my shining examples, speak many languages with less accents? Their classroom is much like my mother's front room was back in the day. They are surrounded by people from other nearby countries. They have the gift of native speakers transiting through their lives on a daily basis. Their learning is immersive as they engage in the conversation of the moment. And yet we continue to think the classroom, a separate entity, is a more effective place. This is the intellectual approach. Again, separation is key.

I can't help but make the observation, that only the human ego would presume to create a better process for language learning than the immersive approach which produces accent less speaking. Now extend this observation. The ego is the ruler of intellect. Both are wedded to separation for their very existence. Separateness, in all its forms, must be superior in the egoic intellectual system than the natural emergence from wholeness that is a story. That emergence is relegated to the trash heap of simple and underdeveloped child's play. Notice that all of the replacements for story are but faded versions of story itself. Without the story there is no need to have theories, spreadsheets, concepts and formulas. Nonetheless we live in a world where these faded versions are held as the highest order of things.

I have shared that I spent many years at the end of my career teaching senior executives leadership skills. Given I had a deep financial background, I would often utilize the construction of a business case as the vehicle for instilling the skill of delivering compelling cases. In this there were two things to teach. One was that the nature of compelling lives not in the construction of a case but in the deliverer himself. Secondly, we would shift all deliveries such that they began and lived from a story. I became well known at my clients as the guy who incessantly taught *"Lead With Story"*.

When a story was used in any presentation you could feel the aliveness in the room. People paid attention to the stories even while their eyelids floated back in their heads at the introduction of a spreadsheet. It was obvious that story was our native structure of delivery. We even calculated how often cases won funding when a story base was used as compared to the spreadsheet-based approach. The story cases performed 3x better. And yet, we would leave and come back some months later and the presenters had reverted to the faded versions approach. Why? It is in the water. We have been educated to believe that our education is a higher form of delivery than the birthright of our very essence. Nobel prizes, tenure, diplomas and certifications all bear testimony to our unconscious and assumptive view of faded versions. Have you ever wondered why folks on the spiritual path believe that well written books and quotes from influential mystics are superior to simple self-inquiry? Are you still wondering?

The way back to your original myth is through tangible movement within your own perception and sense of feel. That trek takes you back to your original story. It does so by throwing off the junk you have onboarded to become an adult. The faded versions that you and I worship every day, while informative, value little in response to the internal turbulence that drives your search. Watch yourself now and let this pointer reflect where you have elevated the complex but lifeless into your story of yourself.

part two

---•◦💮◦•---

The Magic of Story

chapter Nine

———•◦ ⦂◉⦂ ◦•———

story Theory

STORY THEORY is a term I created some years back. As I worked with story and its impact in the corporate world, I began to notice how it belongs to humans in a very special way. Story has a power that is more profound than any other type of communication when it is delivered from its roots. It is as if consciousness itself leaks into the story. I found that story became a container that could straddle the transom from the ineffable to the definable. It could build a bridge people of all walks of life could traverse. Again, I love to remember back to my early childhood when I could read a tale and it would transform into a world of its own. I would spend hours in the solitary of my own room so I could visit, inhabit, my storyland over and over again. This memory seemed critical to the movement of consciousness. It was obvious that the most powerful place I had ever occupied was this childhood story playground. Then I made what seemed a simple observation. Consciousness, in itself, is completely unformed. It then links with a body-mind and animates it in sentience. This first animation is often referred to in spiritual literature as "I Am." It is the first defined version of consciousness, in a unique version, like a snowflake, never like any other.

I now know that humanity in its intellectual self-aggrandizement has focused on the individual quality of the "I Am" but ignored prior consciousness or unity itself. In fact, this view is so suffocatingly enforced that it is assumed that each body that appears is an autonomous creator of its own experience. Yep, I'm talking about ego. This divorce from the juice of life leads to a felt experience of bondage. Many so-called individuals have their intuitive equipment scream out, "Something is terribly wrong!" And they begin to search for what seems like it is missing. But they do so from the ego platform, not realizing that who they have identified with is the separate story of their own identity rather than the ineffable, consciousness itself.

Awakening is simply a phenomenal moment when the whole perception of body-mind life is restored. Often, we refer to the egoic state of assumption as living in the split mind. Why? Because the identification with the body mind and its story as who we solely are obfuscates the pure consciousness that you also are. Your perception locates as though it were the perception of only the body-mind. The pure awareness that operates in a whole manner is simply not recognized. The mind usurps its position and assigns it to its ego self as a much more limited perceptive entity.

When awakening occurs, all is perceived in its original way. This has been called apperception or seeing without a seer. Those who have experienced this permanently often are asked to facilitate others in the same journey. How do we do that? We use pointers and story. There is no way to have the ego extend into consciousness itself. It simply is not possible for a variety of reasons. And so, if the closest experience to awakening itself was the story container of our youth then why not use it to get as near as possible to our original state of undividedness? If the story full of consciousness could enable one to see that they were consciousness itself, then story pointers were a way to get that done.

So, what is the theory? At the bottom of your own story self lies an original version of who you really are. I call this the original myth version of your story. I stole that term from Joseph Campbell! I surmised that if you could reoccupy that original story that you were but millimeters from awakening itself. It appears that consciousness has set up awakening as the magnetic north that pulls all of humanity towards it. If that were the case, then all must pass through storyland to get back home. Is this provable? Not likely. That is why it's a theory. Is it likely to be proven? Probably not. Guess what story pointers are? Yep, they are all the stories used to attempt to deliver you into your original myth.

In simple terms, *Story Theory* is utilizing story to make your way back to the closest moment that you as consciousness itself burst into story. That sounds simple but it is part seeing things clearly and part knowing the intellect cannot hold that movement. Bear with me as I speak about how deep story is a rare thing simply because of our human propensity to fly on the surface. But first, here is a little appetizer that begins to tease the difference out between how we perceive the outside normally and a deeper more unbroken version. Remember that our normal perception is that of the split mind.

I often do a little experiment with seekers in Satsang to demonstrate the split mind. Where is the split? It is the gap we assume separates us from what is out there. I start by asking them to look out at whatever is around them. They are pretty used to doing that. Then I ask them to close their eyes and continue to imagine that they are looking out as they were before. Now comes the moment. I ask them to see the whole picture. See both what is out there and include themselves. How do they do that as their eyes are closed? Perception is not only visual. The perception of awareness is not located within you as the body-mind but rather is located behind consciousness itself. You, and all else, emerge from pure awareness. Simply see all that is out there from the source of emergence. Guess what? That includes you. In this simple moment, the experience of the split mind and the whole mind is teased out.

BUT THE WORLD IS A CLUSTERFUCK

Today's digital and information terrain seems like an endless parade of undifferentiated content. Precisely because of this homogeneity, story and storytelling have become a most popular term. Why is this? Whenever a landscape flattens, it is human nature to kick among the faceless rubble to find the interesting bits. And what is one of the possibilities that might be interesting? That would be a story. You see, stories are more than just a model or a bit of data. They are the natural language of humans across the millenniums, and they partner with human consciousness to create a living field or essence. This authentic story gets noticed in contrast to the deadness of much of the digital scrap pieces that pretend to be alive in the current field of play.

What has been the thrust of the generational millennial movement toward storytelling in all of our digital platforms? It goes something like this. First of all, find your audience and understand what they want. Then construct a story that checks the boxes of the components of their desire. And now learn how to tell your story. Yep, today's storytelling is about how you stand, how you speak, and what you wear. And if you are lucky you might get invited to share your inspirational story in a forum like TED Talks and have your own YouTube video. It's really cool. They put a headset on you, and you look ready to pilot your own Boeing Dreamliner into the sunset. And by current standards you have been dubbed and knighted a storyteller. And now they have a new a better term. An influencer! You can become an ego in separation but a more important one. What's changed in the egoic grab for power due to the insecurity of separation? Nothing but new terms to describe age old behavior.

If you have come to me because you want to follow the storytelling script I have just described, let me save you some time. Don't bother. *Story Theory* is not about telling a story. It is not about how you look, how you stand, and what you wear. It is not about using story to become abundant, wealthy, or to enhance your ego in any way. Ultimately, most folks see story as an object, tool, or a place to arrive. As something you develop and finish. Once you do it becomes available for use over and over again.

But there is a deeper, more alive, possibility that story can deliver. Story can be both a pointer to experience and the field in which that experience takes place. As such, there is no finish or arrival point in this sense of story. Story becomes the place that holds your entire developmental possibility as a human being. It no longer is about an ego using sonar to find the desires of his fellow insecure egos. It is no longer about crafting something that pretends to fill the holes in the undeveloped psychologies in that place we all refer to as a market. It is not about the triangulation from here to the outside.

Story Theory is a term that was created to reflect the deeper use and sense of story. In the tradition of shamans, mentors, creators, and leaders, story has played a much deeper role. Unfortunately, that depth has seemingly been lost in the onslaught of detail that now makes up our lives. And yet, the human need to root in the deeper story can still be felt in all that makes us human. Many of the attempts at storytelling that fall short seem to have this drive for profundity. But as the progenitors of deep story can tell you, the inner work of deep authenticity is the ballast and prerequisite for a story that is compelling. Playing to the outside and hoping that your dysfunctional state of being as it exists today will suffice ignores this deeper possibility. And it is this possibility that *Story Theory* has been created to address.

As luck would have it, I have spent the majority of my life in Southern California. Like many of us, I have had a lifelong love affair with my dogs. I used to have two rescued mastiffs, Bodhi and Lola, who I diligently walked twice a day near the ocean. Now, Bodhi was an excitable character. He would go wild at the very hint that he might get to go on one of his two everyday walks. Our daily habit would be to walk to the end of the hall, wait while I put my shoes on, and launch into our experience. Because of his excitement to get out the door many times he would tug me, sit on me, and incessantly grab my socks and shoes as we would get prepared to leave. I would often chuckle because he just could not see that his excitement actually delayed the very thing that he was excited about doing. But ultimately, we would get out the door and down the road we would go.

I see today's rush toward storytelling in much the same frame. On one hand, we are so excited to launch ourselves into something that will make a difference that we just can't wait to begin telling stories. We intuitively know that story holds something special and indeed we should pursue it with great effort. But we just do not understand what the direction is and what to do with the excitement we feel. So much like Bodhi, we simply expend our effort at whatever is in front of our face. And in this case, we skip the descent into our own authentic roots, the inward journey as it were, in exchange for being in action. And as a result, we still feel the intuition that tells us that we have missed a birthright of a deeper and more profound experience. The West is clamoring for a deeper story but settling for a surface version. To be a storyteller in the digital platform is akin to being the monkey for the organ grinder. And like Bodhi, we opt for monkey status and wallow in the accolades of being the best monkey or teller. Sadly, the reality is that we are a story, and this is the most mystical location for the leap into awakening.

How do we find that more profound experience? We do that by beginning to understand that stories are pointers to a deeper experience within ourselves. By doing so we began to drop the idea that stories are a finished product or a polished concept. What is the difference between pointers and concepts? Pointers deliver you into experience. Concepts are simply an extraction of what you see when you look through the window into the experience of life itself. Storytelling with no true rooting is simply a permanent seat at the window. You get to look but you don't get to play. And if it turns out that you begin to feel the hollowness and inauthenticity of your window seat, you may thrust yourself headlong into the quest to know who you are. This journey is the ultimate human experience. It is for this experience that *Story Theory* has been created. For you are now a seeker. And in the tradition of self-examination across the centuries of humanity, every culture has sought its own version of the journey. Story is the deepest and most natural birthright of contemporary Western culture. Of course, this deep field and essence of living experience is the perfect vehicle for the digital beings of the information age to pursue their version of seekership.

In my lifetime I have had the opportunity to explore many countries. In my mid-30s I was able to live in the country of India for many years while I engaged in my own self-exploration. Of course, every country has its idiosyncrasies and traditions that outsiders immediately adopt. In California it might be the experience of In-N-Out Burger or a taco from Juanita's. And in India the connoisseurship of street chai is equally compelling. One of the first things that anybody notices when arriving in India is the crazy din of the street. And on every street one can find a chai wallah, or fellow who prepares chai, just for his special customers. Of course, within days it is not unusual to have selected your own chai wallah who sees you from a block away and has your drink ready when you arrive. The bad news in all of this is that when you return to your home country it is likely that you will never find a true Indian street chai again. And for certain it will be near impossible to replace your personal relationship with your chai wallah.

Recently, I was told about a place nearby my current home where they make true street chai. You can imagine how excited I was to hear the news. It was only a matter of days before I presented myself at this small French bakery, called Darshan in Encinitas, Southern California.

I could see it on the back counter, the tureen that was so familiar to me that I knew it held the sweet nectar that I could usually only find in India. When it came my turn, I asked for my cup of chai. The woman across the counter sweetly responded that they would be happy to serve me a chai latte.

I immediately asked, "But isn't that tureen full of simple street chai?"

She responded, "Indeed it is, except for here nobody wants to buy chai from the street but rather everyone wants a latte". And in that moment, I recognized our cultural bias of living in the surface story that was special rather than finding the deeper story. And, so often, by taking the shortcut we impoverish ourselves by not participating in a deeper story that would connect us to thousands of years of humans holding hands in the story of street chai.

WE ARE LOSING SOMETHING

Are we actually losing touch with the heritage of deep story? And with it are we losing the possibility to use story in a way that develops our human consciousness? The answer to that is yes and no. Deep story still can be found within the platform of human consciousness. But what has happened is that we have chosen to believe that the delivery of raw content in an age of technological wonder can replace human presence found in deep story. Now, we have not made it a goal to replace the depth of human experience with digital efficiency. It has simply happened. All of us can see the evidence of the shift in our communities, as we know them today. Texting has taken the place of talking. Emails have taken the place of meetings. And even face-to-face computer conversations are deemed equal to meeting in presence. The fact of the matter is that it has just happened. In that happening we have made the unexamined assumption that one thing can replace the other. But can it really?

Some years back I took my son on a long promised five-week vacation to South America. As a child he had begged me to take him to the countries that I knew best. And so, as Michael turned 15, we embarked on a trip to Ecuador, Peru, and Bolivia. I had lived in the Andes of Peru for a couple of years at age 19 and had spent much of my professional life in this region of South America. We decided to spend the week in Ecuador as part of this trip, on the Pacific surf beach of Montanita. It was the largest right-hand break on the Pacific Ocean and for six dollars a night we had found accommodations perfect for a father and son trek.

As luck would have it, we met there an author who spent a month every summer on that beach writing his current novel. Pablo had a wonderful story. He was the son of one of three revolutionaries that included Fidel Castro and Che Guevara. His life had been a function of which part of his family would care take him in his childhood as his father was held in a prison of whichever country the revolution was happening then. My son and I would sit every evening on a balmy beach while Pablo would tell the stories of his life, which included the revolutionary era of the 60's.

This truly was a precious time in our lives.

But I will never forget the question that my 15-year-old boy asked me as we readied to leave our Ecuadorian paradise. "Dad, when we get home where can we go to have talks like that, where can we go to hear more of these stories?" The year was 2000. That moment was like a revelation to me. For I had been raised in the 60's where stories of human events were commonplace. And, over the years, I have never hesitated to find my way to a small plaza or a small bench in any of the countries or cities to which I traveled in order to gather such stories. But, when spoken from the mouth of my child, I recognized that that experience was one that his generation didn't find common. In the 20 years since that time, I have spent much of my life force in trying to point out that we still have within us the heritage of deep story. I have also tried to make clear that if we don't take advantage of the story platform that still remains in our culture, that there may indeed come a time that deep story will have disappeared.

In October 2005 I was lucky to be with one of my lifetime mentors, Ramesh Balsekar. Ramesh was in his 90's, after a long career culminating in being the CEO of the Bank of India. At his retirement, at the age 65, Ramesh began his own journey of self-examination and became the translator for a famous sage, Nisargadatta Maharaj. Some short years after that, Nisargadatta pushed him out of the nest and Ramesh began to speak to his own followers about the inner journey of seekership.

My relationship with Ramesh was a fun one. I had already spent many years in the ashrams of India, as well as exploring my own culture and birthright. I had not come to Ramesh as a seeker, rather simply to sit in his presence. Because of that relationship I was invited to spend afternoons drinking tea and often times discussing financial theory. Ramesh was a graduate of the London school of economics and a long-time CEO of the Bank of India. I was a CPA with a long career in mergers and acquisitions and therefore available to conversations not common in the spiritual world. One afternoon as we sat together Ramesh looked at me with his piercing eyes and said, "Alan, you need to tell the story of seeking in only the way that a Westerner could. In every culture the tradition of seeking will arise. In the beginning it will borrow from other cultures, much as the West has borrowed from the Indian tradition. Now, it is time to write and tell the story of awakening in the mode of the culture itself. I cannot do that, I'm Indian. But you are as American and Western as they come. Your time is now."

Story Theory is the outcome of that conversation. Story pointers are the devices that are most deeply embedded in the Western consciousness and have the possibility to awaken us all. *Story Theory* is dedicated to the use of story as a path of awakening. Some call this path the stages of adult maturity. Others call it the journey of self-development. Whatever you call it, story is the natural possibility that will deliver that outcome.

HUMOR HAS A ROLE

Some time back, as I sat on a heat drenched patio on California summer day, a young man asked me the difference between pointers and intellectual conclusions. I proposed to him that the thing we would most like in that moment would be a pool of fresh cool water standing nearby. And were that the case, we might likely simply jump into it and enjoy that moment of revealed ecstasy as our bodies wallowed in that glorious instant. This would be akin to a pointer. No words, construction or analysis necessary. Simply a jump in the water. However, if upon noticing that such a water hole was nearby, we simply embarked on a conversation about water and its viscosity, we would be entering the world of intellectual conclusions. Notice that many times we are not even able to simply enjoy such a moment of an innate pointer. For, immediately upon jumping in the water, we feel compelled to construct a motive as to why. Really? But we do exactly that most of the time.

All that is happening here is that you have a normal way of viewing the world, a stock story. From the place called "me". What if you did not exist and you found out that someone else was looking through your eyes? Then you found out that same someone else was looking through everyone's eyes at the same time? And then you recognized that this someone else was actually your deepest self? That would be a hoot. You could say that when you thought you were just an individual that you were seeing everything as a small dream. Your dream. Now you find out that you are looking through everyone's eyes at the same time. I guess we could call that the big dream. Awakening goes a little further than that, but that is the first step. Just ask yourself how it would be if you were in the big dream. Because all of the pointers are an attempt to have you move there. So be relentless and never give up. And when that feels serious and you get pissed off, it's time for humorous absurdity. Relentless absurdity is the path. Ready?

chapter ten

———•◦ ◦•———

story is alive!

B Y NOW YOU already have been exposed to a fair amount of story. Why? It is always the same answer. We have been given, or have innocently inherited, restrictive frames of how we look at and experience the world. These become biases which hold such a potent place in our perceptive intellect that they obfuscate all other possible approaches. Story is multi-faceted. It is not cause and effect. It is magic. Go back with me to a childhood experience of a story you read or listened to. One that you really loved. Remember how you could drop into living one piece of the story and then dropping out and sliding right back into another? Dragons would be flying around your bedroom and then suddenly you were floating in a sunlit forest of cooing birds and strange, talking flowers. Crafting a story experience is a meta skill. It dissolves how you have likely concretized your world as an adult. Things have become black and white. Things have become polarized. But this is not the truth of the matter. The inclination to create the magic of story is a birthright for all humans. Then sadly, it gets weeded out. Let's get it back!

One of my favorite childhood stories was Peter Pan. My mother bought me a book of this tale when I was 4 or 5 years old. Peter had endless adventures. There was Tinkerbell the fairy, who flitted around in thin air, and the crocodile with a clock ticking ominously in its stomach. This creature wanted to eat Captain Hook. Over and over again I would read this tale and immerse myself in it. I would craft a kind of boat out of the blankets in my bedroom. I would invite Peter and the boys into the boat. We would listen very carefully and if we heard the clock ticking, we knew the alligator and Captain Hook were nearby. The story melted into my bedroom and my imaginary friends went on adventures with me. There literally was no difference between the characters that populated my mind and the ones that played in my bedroom. In fact, they all seemed ever so more alive than the adults in a little boys' world. Adults who seemed intent on having no fun.

Now, many of you might contend that story itself is a construction. And that contention is correct. But, at its deepest level, it is a construction of a special kind - it is the first construction. It is so basic that we knew our very own special story, as small children. Now take a moment and go back in time when you were reading fairy tales and the like. You will remember how vivid that experience was. And in that first iteration, the story could be said to live within the emotional and experiential field that we really are. Or we could say that story itself holds that very field. Either one works just fine, for it begins to tease out the difference between our assumptive knee-jerk action to live in our head versus the experience that we truly are. Many times, you will hear me speak of the "weather" in understanding what is around you at any one point in time. The emotional and experiential field is that very weather. You are within that field or weather but assuming you are separate. So first we get that separate "you" to notice what is around you. Then we aim at letting you and it melt into one. Where did that "you" and its weather or fields arise from? Yep, I have spoken about the first story "I Am". This is our first moment of the sense of presence and animation. As a child we live directly in that essence until it is fastidiously weeded out to shape us for adulthood. When I ask you to go back and remember fairy tales and the like, that is not the same as the first story or original myth. But the energy of being so close to the "I Am' moment is who we are, and it fuels all else. Certainly, more so when we are children.

I often call story "the music of the intellect". As you ponder what music is, think about how we break it down into notes and symbols. But is that music? No, it is a movement in experience. The notes have no beginning and no ending because they are part of a moving stream. Of what? Why, any child will tell you. The stream of music. Story is like music. You can construct it from the outside in and indeed it appears to have pieces. This is the way the vast majority of humans hold that life happens. But Mozart played from the inside out. His first experience was the unbroken melody of artistry. Then he figured out how to portray that emergence as constructed music so others could access it.

Would they access it to the core of where it had emerged? Only if they could reverse the current and direction from which they accessed it in the first place. From sheet music, or map, to music is but a faint echo of the natural flow from music to map.

The descent into story is exactly the same exercise. It looks like it has parts once rendered and delivered into play. But it emerged from where there are no parts. Much like writing this book looks to all the world as an amalgamation of parts, it is not. From pure awareness to story. Why else would a seeker listen to a sage? Story is the same. We have broken down language into letters and symbols. But story, like music, moves within you with no notice of the boundaries of symbol. Story learning is a tautology. A famous poet once asked a child the color of a leaf. The answer was immediate, "Why, it's green." The second question followed, "Why is it green?" The answer again was immediate, "Because it's green". You see green does not have a why and any child knows that.

In order to answer that question in an adult way we have to teach children that all that can be cognized has a cause. The ego is a concept of the same ilk. The need to engage causally is the first dose of the fatal disease called "I". That is the unease you live with every day. If it can be caused, it can and will die. And you know that you cannot die even in your assumptive conviction, given by societal intellectual inoculation, that you can. And though you have no clue who you are, you live the dissonance of inauthenticity. Because you do know, you just don't know how to access it. That is the seeker's journey.

Note that the simple knowing that green is green and uncaused is the same condition of the pure awareness that you really are. All that makes you uneasy lives in the notion of separation, beginnings and endings and death as a possibility. But green cannot die any more than you can. The juice of non-separation has no boundary lines. No entrance, no exit.

SEEKERS LOOK FOR THE MAGIC

So, what is a seeker and why do I use that term? Seeking is something that we see every day. Sometimes it is a captain of industry building a multinational corporation. Sometimes it is an artist creating digital art. And other times it is simply a child reaching for a cookie. It is human nature to seek. However, let's narrow our definition of seeking to the universal and driving force from which all of these emanations arise. It is the naturally embedded nature of consciousness to reveal itself to itself. And the seeking to which I refer is the inner version in which the question never varies. It is and always is, "Who am I?" In the outer versions of seeking there is a moment of peace that one finds when the desire to obtain has been quenched. And before another desire can take its place there is no seeking. And this moment is often the only felt peace that one will ever experience. And often it becomes like a drug where everything aims for that single moment, and then everything again for the next one. The only difference between seeking for objects and seeking for awakening is that awakening can be permanent. In fact, it is your natural state. Instead of continually needing to achieve something to quench the latest desire, desire itself is seen through.

For millenniums, paths have made themselves known and an internal seeking has given some few lucky souls a standing in permanent peace. And people have flocked to avail themselves of these various paths. Why? They have been bitten by the seekers' bug. And why would they be so driven? What would make them know that the fleeting moments of emptiness and peace could become a permanent state? They know because intuitively it is their very birthright and home. They know because they feel it. Their constant exercise in futility begins to wear on them. And in this process, a revealing begins to arise. This is the very nature of life itself.

Story pointers are just a contemporary version of these myriads of paths that have gone before. Why is it important? Because story is the basis of human interchange. And if we are to have a relevant path in today's platforms of technology and emergent global culture, story is a perfect device. Not the kind of story, as I said before, that you find in print. But the kind of story in which you live, and which is the first iteration of whom you are. For it is from this very first moment of story that it is possible to step back into the essence of consciousness that you are.

If you look around, it is easy to see that most humans are on some version of a seeker's journey. With so many objects of pursuit, it is apparent that we are all looking for something. In fact, the common denominator of humanity seems to be a search so desperate that most people go through life in a state of perpetual bondage to this seeking. Looking everywhere except inside themselves, they cobble together a life that they imagine will be better if they succeed in changing the scenery.

In some cases, this search for satisfaction through external acquisition and achievement becomes so frustrating that the individual finally turns inward and dedicates his or her life to being a spiritual seeker. But the problem is the same for every seeker—and we are all seekers, regardless of our goals and the context of our efforts. We become trapped in a state of dissatisfaction and frustration of our own design, which is called "the seeker's hole". And we become completely convinced that unless we do all the right things, we will be stuck down there forever. We struggle like hell to get out by any means we think will work, never realizing what is responsible for keeping us in there, much less how to get out.

But here is the problem with this kind of seeking. We continue to assume that we, as an autonomous author of our own journey, can find something. This will never yield a result, rather only the continued frustration that fuels a seeker. It is not until we see that the assumption we make is flawed, and we turn to ourselves as consciousness and awareness itself, that internal spiritual movement that obviates the internal turbulence begins.

GRANDPA AND MAGIC

I often speak of my grandpa and I invite you to walk with me in your version of that kind of experience. The magic childhood was that the world around us was ready to explore. In fact, we tracked it. That was long before our adult ego pushed out our exploratory world and replaced with a to do list. Moving through life was like the weather. Yep, here we are back to weather or fields of emotion and experience if you like. They are as real as what we normally think is weather. In my town the eucalyptus aroma wafted through the morning air. Orange blossoms played their soprano role to the bass of the Australian trees. Sights and sounds are like the weather to a child. As a leadership resource in the corporate world, I would often teach, or reteach, how does the weather feel even in a boardroom? One of the main impediments to your search is the adult hold on life which pushes everything out as the ego takes up space. Pretty soon the only weather is in your head. Let's go back and reclaim our natural gift. How do we begin to make this shift in our life?

One of my original drivers in imbedding this approach was to use story in a way that I had acquired through a lifetime of unrequited mentorship. It certainly began with my grandfather, who sat me on his knee and molded stories of the Greek philosophers into versions that a four-year-old could understand. Later, as I have mentioned, men such as Stephen Covey, Milton Friedman, and Peter Drucker would appear as mentors. They, too, immediately recog-

nized both the gift of story that I carried and its importance to our world at large. And they tailored their input
and influence to leverage the use of story. They taught me
to use story much like a seasoned coach would teach a bud-
ding superstar to perform in his natural sport.

Later, as I engaged in my personal journey, Osho and
Ramesh Balsekar became spiritual mentors and deepened
my sense of how story could be a container for awareness.
It was at the feet of all of these great mentors, my mother
included, that I more than understood the sense of story.
Yes, I actually held and was the story. I could see that the
gritty, tangible, and rooted story was an actual living container that offered a possibility of self-discovery that I had
yet to see at its fullest. When I was small, the message was
always that I was "too much". Yet, armed with story, that
same intensity was greedily gulped down by those same
voices. Look into your own life. Where was it that you were
allowed to wallow in the simplicity of story? How did that
feel? What was the weather? You know this place and returning to your original birthright is the activity that all
pointers intend to create for you.

For those who know my writing, you know there is
nothing better than a grandpa story. In the days when I
was just a tyke of about four years, I would wait vigilantly
for my grandpa to come home from his job at the Pontiac
dealer in San Diego. Once home, he and I would often disappear into the beautiful backyard that my grandmother
cared for so lovingly. And while it seemed to me that I had
been transported to a magical land of dreams and stories,

my grandfather used this time to pour his soul into his oldest grandchild. One of the things he would stress was the difference between what he called "description" and story. I suspect that this was a little unusual for most four-year-old's but with my grandfather it was a grand adventure that we shared.

One particular day as the sun was setting over Mission Bay, my grandfather and I sat under the orange trees and watched as the butterflies of late afternoon made their appearance. As this began to happen my grandfather said, "Alan, tell me what a butterfly is to you". Of course, I described to him the size, the color, the wings and design. And when I was done grandpa looked at me and said, "But Alan, I didn't feel how the butterfly moves as it darts from leaf to leaf. And I don't know how you feel about butterflies, do you love them?"

Immediately I responded, "But grandpa, how do I make butterflies move for you and let you know I love them?"

In that moment, my grandpa told me something that I would hear many times in the years that came. "If you want to give people the short answer, just describe what you think or what you see. But if you want to make a butterfly move for them and know how a little boy like you loves them, then tell them a story."

And so, my grandpa and I made up a story. We picked my favorite butterfly and named him Norman. And for the rest of my life, we added to that story. Whenever we would meet someone named Norman, we would giggle like two little children, for we had named a butterfly that very same thing. But the main point is that grandpa was right. If you want to create the possibility that someone really feels what you want them to feel, knows what it is like to love a butterfly, then tell them a story. How do you make those around you know that you love butterflies? Tell that story and watch how you become smaller in the story, so your beloved butterfly has all the room he needs. When you step into your essence of original myth, your story terrain will adjust to the natural perception of consciousness itself. Wow!

Oak Tree Story

Fast forward to the age of 11. By then my relationship with my grandpa had morphed and matured. But what was the constant? Our relationship was driven by the insistence that our stories were vibrant and robust. In this little story it seems that Grandpa is talking about the maturity of becoming a man. And in a way, indeed he was.

By age 11 I had moved to Corona, California where the old washes were littered with giant oak trees. I created a Christmas business by shooting mistletoe out of those old trees and bagging them up for door-to-door sale. In the summer, the desert heat of the day would pound those trees all day long. And then the temperature would begin to decline, and the trees would pour out the perfume of tree-ness that I loved so dearly. Those trees were a tangible part of my everyday life and I loved them. You can be sure my Grandpa knew that. Notice how he made that the real anchor for his teaching.

Now, I have a fairly profound emotional base. As a kid I had effusive emotional eruptions and did not know what to do with all that energy. At about the age of 11, my grandpa saw how I struggled. He could see that I felt lost, overwhelmed, and felt like something was terribly wrong. Sure enough, there came a moment when he stepped in. He gathered me up the minute he felt there was an opening and told me the story of the old oak tree.

"Chuck, (our secret nickname for me)," he said, *"The power and strength of a man is often misunderstood. Men are encouraged to show emotion, similar to the way that women do. We're expected to insert ourselves into every kind of dramatic event. But let me tell you, that isn't how men work.*

Our most powerful emotional aspect is called rooting. And sadly, it is seldom seen or mentioned. That is our real strength. It is not in obvious broad stroked actions taken, but in the position held. There is more power in the unexpressed than in the weakness of an explosion once it has passed.

We are like old oak trees in the face of the largest tsunami. We stand firmly in our power while the raging of the water of life passes over, under, and around our steadfast rooting. And when it's all done, we smile at ourselves, we smile at the trees next to us, and occasionally, we even wink. Is it emotional? Oh yeah. Is there much to say or generate? Nope. Just the wordless sharing with the other oak trees that stand with us, individually but bonded in the experience of our stance.

And when those around us fly into the chaos of displayed emotion, they are often, without knowing, looking for the comfort of the old, rooted oak tree. Give them that silent comfort, even if you are being blamed for the very weather they are creating. Then find another of your tree mates and smile, and maybe even wink."

The magic of story is to mentor yourself in your journey. What are your stories when you make them live and wallow in who you are? You see, your stories are the first expression of who you really are. The ineffable consciousness of your original identity pours out into your body, mind and environment. How close must you be when you live one click away from who you really are? Yep. Enter in the front of the story and exit out the back. Then let the perceptive perfection of your original awakened state make itself known.

chapter eleven

———•◦ ⋯◦⋯ ◦•———

modes of construction

O NCE THE SENSE of being in the story starts to arise within the experiential field, a large part of the transformational process rests in noticing what is there. This running thread of mental story is part of the human attempt to give the ego a sense of felt security. In the movement of transformation, at some point in time, this attempt must cease. For when the mind is engaged in both the past and the future, the victim becomes the present. How often do you notice that you are called back to something that is happening right here and right now and you weren't even present? Notice as this happens. This is a marker in the experiential field informing you of where the story is really located. The fact of the matter is that the only security within consciousness that the human form can find is in being present here and now. By conflating the mental holding of what is believed to be here and now with what actually is, the possibility of being here and now is nullified.

Story Theory and its pointers all rest in being present. Over time the sense of being present deepens and the particulars that one notices begin to lose their significance. But until that begins to happen, the process starts with the noticing of what is in the field of presence. Here is a pointer designed to simply make you aware of how you might see the world as a result of your screen of understanding. That is to say, every unique body-mind has it's likely preference of cognitive extraction from the entirety of what is.

All human beings seem to be constructed with certain preferential ways of on-boarding understanding. In essence, these ways of understanding will dictate how a story lives within your field of experience. Years ago, I was exposed to a field called neural linguistic programming or NLP. Within this field they were three process modes of on-boarding or understanding the experience of story. These were labeled as visual, auditory, and kinesthetic. As I understood these modes, I could readily see that I was highly attuned to the kinesthetic mode. This meant that I understood the story that I lived primarily in terms of feeling. You will notice in my writing and my speaking that I use many feeling words. In fact, I speak often of felt experience which clearly leans in the direction of kinesthetic understanding. The other two fields were visual and auditory which is simply seeing and hearing. The majority of the world population is considered to be visual, which is easy to see in the world around us. And, of course, we cannot help but notice the high volume of auditory learning in our worlds of music and cinematic presentation.

It seems that every human has his or her own combination of modes of understanding. In describing these particular three there is not a presumption that one would reside in just one of these modes, but rather a combination of the three. Additionally, this is simply an approach nested in my sense of pragmatic occurring. In other words, it is just a story I use which may or not be helpful to you. So, this is not to say that some other version of understanding modes of learning would not work just as well. But what is important is to notice what your own access points might be.

Society is anxious to tell you how to learn. And it is quite possible that you have become accustomed to utilizing an on-boarding mechanism that is not your strongest. Look outside yourself and begin to notice which elements of what you experience resonate in the strongest manner for you. Ultimately, the *Story Theory* journey takes you to the original story essence of who you are. The access to this essence, your original story, will be held and most easily understood in the mode of understanding that is already natural for you. Is it visual, is it auditory, or is it kinesthetic? Quite likely you may have never noticed that you have a strong capability in one area and a lesser in another. This then will be a new exercise. But understanding your natural composition in modes of learning will allow you to access the pointers that lead you to your transformational basement.

The very act, the beginning to notice your own modes, is an exercise in being present. In order to understand which of these combinations is strongest, you cannot help but peer into the present. It is in this exercise that you will begin to notice that some things resonate stronger than others. And you will also begin to notice which of these things are most comfortable for you as well. And when you want to engage in letting a pointer locate you within experience, you will naturally hold that pointer in the mode that is most comfortable and resonant for you.

ARE YOU VISUAL, AUDITORY, OR KINESTHETIC?

Some time back I moved to the Big Island of Hawaii. I wanted to return to a farming style area similar to what I had enjoyed as a child. My new place is out in a remote area with papayas, coconuts and just plain foliage as far as the eye can see. It also includes wildlife. Mongoose, frogs, wild pigs and birds of all kinds roam wild. The birds are so active here that many ask if I live in an aviary. Because I still take the occasional corporate call, this background music of the birds is most noticeable. It isn't often that corporate decisions are made with this backdrop. This is a great situation to observe how different modes of learning, modes of construction, are evident. You can do this sleuthing on others and yourself.

For example, here's how it goes. When the business meeting begins the visual folks often say, "Wow, those birds are something. Your place must be bursting with color. I'll bet you can see them flying all over the place." The auditory folks will say something like, "My goodness, that sounds like a symphony. You must simply enjoy all that great music all day long." Now, I don't need to hunt far for a kinesthetic comment because I represent that tribe. My typical response is, "You should feel it out here. I'm tucked into a sunshine drenched merry band of warmth, cozy beauty, sound and color." If you pay attention to others and to yourself, you will likely know what the most comfortable version of expression is for you. I can go back to my childhood and remember fairy tales and how they felt. To this day, I cannot watch anything that includes a dog dying. It hurts too much and that feeling arises from how I hold story.

WHERE IS MY KEY?

A favorite story of mine is one of the many told about a humorous character believed to have lived in the Middle Ages—a Sufi mystic and philosopher by the name of Mullah Nasruddin. It seems that one night the mullah lost the key to his house. He decided to call all his friends together so that they could engage in a mass search for it. When they all gathered, he led them to the busiest of all the local markets. In one of the most densely trafficked areas, he got down on his hands and knees and began to dig under a streetlamp, digging into every corner for the key. The others diligently followed suit until, finally, one of his friends looked up and asked, "Mullah, is this where you lost your key?"

"No," the Mullah immediately replied. "Not at all. But the light is brighter here. Look how well-lit it is!"

The seekers' journey to the original story is best done utilizing what is most natural to that seeker himself. It makes sense that your original story would be rendered in the mode that is your authentic own. In fact, that mode will be a fundamental piece of the story itself. This is another way of saying that it is more intelligent to look for a lost key where it was left rather than where it is well lit. As you can see, "well lit" means an entirely different thing to the visual person than it would to the auditory soul. In the very looking one has no choice but to be present to the experience that is arising rather than the mental story that so often derails the very possibility of looking.

Awakening is a return to your original perception. You know that your current perceptive funnel is based on a notion of you as an autonomous entity. That is what we are returning from. Retracing the path until we arrive back to the fork where we veered into separation as a way of being is our first move. Your most powerful self lives within your most powerful stories. Let those stories magnetize you back to where they locate within your felt experience. The deep notion of story and the theory attached is that the retracing can be done in the story chain. Your processed self, or ego, would like you to look for the key where the light is best. That kind of spirituality simply carries all of the assumptions that have you feeling in bondage right into the search itself. Does that make sense? I have a flat tire. Let's just slap another one on. Oh, the flat is still on the car? No worries. Just glue the new on right on top! The ego cannot be a part of the search party looking for where the ego is not.

Discover your mode of understanding. Don't simply use whatever is there. When you find it, it will bring you to the here and now. It will reveal to you what in a story is the most like you. Now when we go looking for our stories, we know what kind of a sense they likely will be rendered within. And all of this is intended to point you to your own sense of being.

chapter twelve

───•◦ ⚬◯⚬ ◦•───

The Three Levels of Story

A S WE GO along, a major pointer in story theory is to hold the world from the inside out. What do I mean by that? Most theories, which are simply attempts to see what works, look at life happening from the outside in. In essence, the basic idea is to create a map that sees what the terrain looks like from the outside. It is then up to you to migrate that point of view into the internal experience of life itself. But there are obstacles to this approach actually working. The first is that most folks do not distinguish between a description of the territory and the territory itself. They believe that they have taken on board something of tremendous value. But they do not understand that it needs to be migrated into their actual experience. They then practice migrating it into their map but not into the territory of experience. Resultantly, most human beings do not develop a competency to do this migration.

This unseen behavior operates within most folks. And stories and their use fall squarely within this pattern. Stories are received but then not utilized in order to navigate the internal experience of those that have heard them. They simply form a part of the content that one holds and often believes is living somewhere in experience. Unfortunately, this is not the case. It is just another of our assumptions that neatly make up our assumptive state. We often hear the expression that we need to "be present". This is just another version of what I have just described. Why would someone call that out? Because they notice that when engaging with another person that they just don't seem to be there. Where are they? Let me submit a possibility. They are roaming around in the map or story that they believe is somehow their experience. They have over the years stored stories and maps and live in that mental terrain as an honest but unconscious expression of thinking they are present. But to any who experiences them it is obvious that they are not.

In essence, that is the difference between a model and a pointer. A model is part of the map or held story. A pointer asks one to find the sense of what is being pointed to within experience itself. Knowing that you are a story yourself and are in a story are my ways of asking you to live inside experience and connect what appears in your experience to what I am pointing to. Another way of saying this is, "What does it feel like inside your story?" "What is the weather?" As you walk through your experience or story, how do the pointers you have heard look within your internal terrain? And then when you notice your version, immediately throw away mine. Your experience rendered into your holding is the gold standard of *Story Theory*.

By doing this you will notice that you have no choice but to be present to what is happening right now. How could it be otherwise? To find your sense of these pointers in your own experience you have to diligently watch your own experience. In so doing you will gradually develop the muscle that has you present to the "now" where the action actually is located. And you will begin to see the models and stories that you hold for your life are really simply a mental escape. In short, you will begin to actually know what is happening and what is the delusion of impact that is held as consensus reality by most humans on the planet.

Another, more esoteric, way to explain this is to understand that what is being pointed towards is raw presence or consciousness, not yet in action. That is the essence of "here and now". We could call that infinite nothingness. Intellectual approaches in the path of knowledge attempt to target that "infinite nothingness" by the use of a model or story. It starts on the outside and attempts to pierce consciousness. What are the chances of hitting the target "infinite nothingness" in reality by use of a concept? Zero. A pointer, on the other hand attempts to push you into the water itself and have you recognize that the "here and now" is that "infinite nothingness". Now the action can move from the inside out and the so-called location of the target "infinite nothingness" is no longer needed. You are actually there, and you are that.

Imagine that we are making our way through the experience of life and we begin to notice some things. We notice that when someone communicates a story to us that some are more powerful or land truer than others. Remember that we cognize everything into a story, so all communication is story based. Then it occurs to us that we could share our observations, but we have to render it into a form to share it. What are our choices, the differences, and how do we explain them? Well, generally it seems that there are three different kinds of stories that live in certain ways. Why don't we call those levels? Are there really three levels? Probably not, but we will let those who want to engage in our same noticing the freedom to define the differences in any way they want. Because we know that we are simply pointing to experience and saying, "Hey we see some differences". And if you can describe ten levels that is great. But remember that explanation is simply your map of the territory within which you know there are felt differences.

What are the three levels of story? The first is what I call the object level. This kind of story is like a package. Put the pieces in the box, wrap it properly, and give it to someone that will take it. Typically, this is the most common sense of story. We see it in most of our media. In fact, we worship folks that live in this most rudimentary space as storytellers. That means that they are the very best at boxing and packaging. But wait, I thought story theory promised something much more profound. Glad you asked, indeed it does. It would be silly to aspire to be a storyteller when you could live at the authentic source of story and, in fact, be that very authenticity.

The second level I call the platform level. This is simply when someone seeks to have you replace a story you already hold with a new one. This works with individuals and groups. You most often see this kind of story use in politics and other conversations dubbed "important". Why is that? Because this level is asking for you to make an internal move. Most of the time this internal move is not all that monumental, for you are exchanging one part of the map for another. Remember, you believe you actually live there. But we now know you do not. But it still calls out tremendous emotion. We have linked our sterile stories and lifeless map to our emotions because we believe in some way, they are real. Thus, the platform level is one of creating an emotional motivation to move from the platform of an old story to a new one. And when more folks stand on the new platform than the old one, the new version is in dominance. In dominance where? In the map.

The third, and deepest, level of story is what I call the basement level. It is at this level that the recognition that you and all that arises within your experience function as a story. It does this because you automatically cognize it to be so. But, if you and the story live at the source of cognition and are aware of that, then change is possible. It is within this climate that one begins to look directly at experience as it arises in this very moment. It is here that pointers to experience begin to matter. For instead of changing a held story located somewhere in the map of memory and counting that to mean something, the particulars of now are looked at as story pieces. It is in this field that transformation and awakening are possible. If the elements and particulars of who you are are but a construction, then the possibility for reassembly remains forever available in this very moment. Your original myth story lives at the basement level. It broaches the gap from pure consciousness itself to the perfect constructed story of you. Your journey is to retrace your steps by going through the front door of constructed story and emerging into pure consciousness. To do that one must be at the basement level.

In the first two levels of story all that is available is simply a horizontal move from one story to another. And when that move is made a new story occupies a place in the map where the old one used to live. We could call this a translative action. This is not to say that story translation isn't useful, for it does help one to hold stories in a lighter matter learning that it is possible to change one story for another. But, ultimately, transformation requires a descent into the profundity of who one is. And it is only possible to live in rooted authenticity if one lives their story where roots are actually found. All of the *Story Theory* pointers are intended to open the doorway for you to enter into your own experience.

As you know, I have worn out the notion that awakening is a retracing resulting from misidentification. But notice here how the levels of story are, in essence, that same retracing. The object level is the most surface. The platform level has the feel of something happening but that is only the result of our conflation of map with territory. And the third level, the basement, is the only place the magic of the gap between presence and construction happens. Which is the deepest internal version? The basement version, of course. Do you see the retracing? Do you see how the object level, the most used, is the natural growth outward from original myth? You will find this retracing to original presence in all awakening movement.

I always say that presence is presence. This retracing process is one that I used constantly in the corporate world of leadership. In fact, I detailed the Original Myth practice earlier in our journey. It is true that most executives weren't interested in stepping past the original myth story into spiritual transformation, or at least that is what they would say. But they all knew that presence was the marker of a great leader and they did not hesitate to follow back to the original myth space in pursuit of that presence. I can remember fondly my conversations with Stephen Covey about this very subject. My concern at the time was that I was somehow inauthentic in using this pointer with executives when its ultimate possibility was a spiritual awakening, not simply the explosion of presence within the egoic corporate platform. Stephen would say, "Alan, isn't the process the same except for the last step?" I would say, "Yes". "And Alan, aren't you the one who claims that the spiritual journey can happen on the corporate terrain as easily as any other?" And I would say, "Yes". "Then Alan, why would you deny anyone the movement in their own journey to whatever whistle stop to which they can arrive?" And I would say, "But shouldn't I be real and call it out as spiritual?" And Stephen would say, "Do the words matter? They signed up for the corporate development journey. Give it to them".

Since those days I have never worried about parsing the words and terms that seemingly describe any life journey. From the infinite nothingness proceeding out into constructed consciousness the pointers have flowed, being spoken in the way they wish and meeting those where they are in the journey. Authenticity lived, not mentally processed, has become the way forward. Let it become the way forward in the journey within which you tread.

chapter thirteen

The story model Ratio

M ANY YEARS ago, when I was a young executive, I noticed something in my interactions, both one on one and in meetings. It all started innocently enough. I had graduated from college at Brigham Young University in 1977. I had performed so well in my final years that I had been hired by Price Waterhouse, their only hire out of 180 interviews. PW had not interviewed at BYU for many years and my year was their first time back. Not only was I lucky but everyone was rooting for me. That said, I was one of 36 newbies in the Los Angeles office and there was not much to distinguish me from the janitor let alone the other highly qualified comrades of mine. It turns out that there was a distinguishing story that I would have never imagined that came in to play. Let me give you some background.

As you know by now, I largely grew up in Corona, California in the 60's. It was a small town of about ten thousand folks and our towns livelihood was growing and distributing oranges. My very first job at 14 was working in the packing house. In a small village like this everyone is part of the family. The kids in town, like me, were referred to as Sunkist kids. All of our product was part of the large national Sunkist cooperative. Our groves covered the largest spread of land in the country. The big boss or chairman of the Sunkist Cooperative was a man named George Hampton, Mr. Hampton to all of us kids.

We had moved to Corona when I was in the 3rd grade so my Dad could work as the controller with Sunkist. We were part of the family. One of my favorite memories of Mr. Hampton was the 4th of July ritual he created for the kids in town. Our little city had been built around a circular racetrack constructed for its first race in 1913. The racing only lasted 3 years as it was financially unsuccessful and in the last race a tragic crash killed 3 people, including the driver. Most every child knew this story by heart. Because the racetrack named Grand Boulevard circled the old town it became central to Corona and gave it the nickname the Circle City. Well, Mr. Hampton decided to start a sweet custom using Grand Boulevard every July 4th. He had a beautiful Peirce Arrow car and, on that day, would bring it out and take the kids in town for a jaunt around the circle. He was a beloved figure, certainly among the kids.

In a town like this the kids are important. So much so that when one leaves the city for the bigtime it is an event. I remember, after graduating from college, coming back to visit the packing house. Their little worker bee was a success. Tears welled up in the eyes of the women packers, who always brought all the boys' homemade burritos daily, at my success. Many could not speak an entire sentence in

English, but I was one of their own.

Guess what? That little story came into play at my first job at Price Waterhouse. It seems like yesterday that I walked into the office with 35 other greenies shaking in our boots. After 3 weeks of intensive training, we were all placed in a common room where we would work. It was obvious to all that we were but cogs in the machine and hardly distinguishable one from another. This was a very stiff atmosphere. We were all coached that you never talked to a partner. In fact, my first day I said "Good morning" to a partner and was called into HR for the correction. Wow, this was not how I was used to dealing with folks in a small town. It was just a couple days later that I received word that Ray Johnson, the managing partner, had requested to see me. In the staff room we were all sure that my gaffe likely meant the end of my multiday career at the company. Nothing could have prepared me for the purpose of the meeting.

As I walked into Mr. Johnson's office, he invited me to sit across from him at the desk. He looked directly into my eyes and said, "I wanted to meet you simply to make sure I know who you are. You see, I received a call earlier today from Mr. Hampton. You know that Sunkist is one of our most important clients. Mr. Hampton told me that I was now lucky enough to have one of his kids. He also told me that he expected me to treat you as I would someone who had excited an entire city by getting a job at our company."

Wow. I was dumfounded. Mr. Johnson, seeing my response, asked if he could give me some advice. I nodded yes, as words were not happening yet at this point. "Alan", he said, "until I received Mr. Hampton's call you would have been but one of the many suits I see in the halls. But once I heard the story, I was frankly excited to meet you. I am sure you know by now that excitement is not exactly falling from the trees around here. Remember this in your career. When a story replaces an object, we all are enlivened." Mr. Johnson went on to assign me to the IBM account, the plum of all assignments, and this one happening became the platform for my meteoric career.

I suppose lack of experience can be a good thing. It was at this point that I began to watch how folks in business reacted to how things were packaged in meetings and conversations. This was the beginning of *Story Theory*. The Story Model Ratio is simply an observation. Remember, we use pointers to replace other stories that have you living in a mistaken identity. The simple act of watching activity around you with a new story in mind is the opening for that change. We call this building a living understanding. The new story simply opens a perception that otherwise has never been seen.

From that day at PW, I began to notice that when someone would use a story those in the room seemed to charge up. Yep, tracking the emotional weather in the room, one could feel the energy rise. Then when the conversation began to be delivered in models, graphs, spreadsheets and theories the eyes in the room began to glaze over. The palpable energy of the story moment was now leaking out of the room. If, however, a next story was introduced the energy immediately began to recharge this room again. I watched this over and over again. This noticing was a central staple in my corporate leadership teaching later in my career. I was known as the "Lead with Story" guy when it came to presentation and case work.

I am sure you are asking what all of this has to do with awakening. I would ask the same thing. The goal of pointers is to do a couple of things. You already know these. First, you need to replace one story with a new living version. The second is to bring you as close to your real essence as possible to the consciousness that is who you really are. Remember, the only thing you can say for sure about yourself is that you exist. That sense of existence funnels itself through all of us as body-minds and creates the weather you are tracking. The closer you are to source; the more energy of existence is funneled through. We can all feel the palpability of our own existence. As you wander away from source the signal gets weaker, and your eyes roll back in your head until you fall asleep!

This pointer is intended to encourage you to watch and feel this such that you begin to have a different perception. A perception that is connected to who you really are. Remember that I have said that there is a gap that the intellect cannot cross into the intuition. Form cannot reach formlessness for it is emergent from exactly that. What gets us closer to the gap? Story. It is the first arising of consciousness. This pointer tells you to wallow in story, use story, feel story and see how close it brings you to yourself. The story model ratio is in play. Watch and see for yourself.

chapter fourteen

New pair of jeans

I F YOU FEEL like much of what we consider here is somewhat repetitive, you would be correct. Remember that the wisdom path is iterative. Why is that? Because we hold on to our story conceptions of what we believe to be true in a very stubborn and tangible way. Much like deconstructing a brick wall, pointers are digging out various pieces of the cracked concrete between the bricks. A little piece falls out here and another there. Soon the bricks come tumbling down.

This chapter's pointer is a direct hit on our stubbornness of thought and how we unconsciously use our death grip on our most beloved concepts. Even in the face of wanting to move into something new, we egoically slip, many times at the very last second, into our old pattern. It is as though we can recite and even broadcast the new revelatory pointer but the old theme music that runs underneath in our automatic behavior ends up being our marching music.

This pointer brings with it a wonderful treat. We get to meet Mulla Nasruddin again. We aren't sure if Nasruddin is a real historical figure or not. You can find references to him as a 13th century figure in present-day Turkey. He was considered a Sufi sage but in a very special way.

In 1990, again, I made my way to India to absorb all I could from a beautiful man and mentorlike influence named Osho. Here I was first introduced to the Nasruddin stories via the oral style of storytelling. As I tell these stories you will notice I simply pass them on as I hold them from my time hearing them from Osho. He would tell us that Nasruddin was a Sufi and that Sufis are a very playful bunch. In fact, what we would call blasphemy is the very basis of the Nasruddin stories. Osho would often say that the Sufi's simply made Nasruddin up. The Sufi way is to make fun of yourself as a path of prying the glue of identity away from your egoic self-importance. Osho would say that Nasruddin was symbolic of human stupidity. And that he knew it and laughed at it. Whenever Nasruddin carries on like a stupid man he is just joking at you and at humanity at large.

Now this trait of transparent thought evidently showed itself in childhood. In elementary school one of his teachers made the attempt to broaden the narrow concepts of her class. To do this she asked each of the students to write an essay on foreigners. Each of the children wrote what you would suppose was an acceptable essay. Each of them except, you guessed it, Nasruddin. The hard-bitten young man's entire essay was a single sentence, "All foreigners are bastards."

This response shocked the young teacher but spurred her to increase her energy to broaden the horizons of her students. In the next lecture she proceeded to expound on

Greek architecture, Roman law, Italian poetry, Russian novels, Chinese philosophy and African sculpture. She then asked the students to write another essay on foreigners. She was delighted at the result as the kids really responded well. As she reviewed the papers, she came to that of Nasruddin. With anxiety and a beating heart she prepared to read his essay. It said, in full, "All foreigners are bastards. Some are cunning bastards."

I notice often that much of what is said in pointer style is met with simple rejection or the insistence that we argue about whether or not the pointer is true. But remember, again, pointers make no attempt to be true, but rather reveal where your crystallized identification might be hiding among your concrete like perceptive frame. In fact, it is as if the release of a long-held belief would rob you of some deep essence of who you really are. I suppose this could be true if you believe you are your story, but hopefully, we have eliminated that as a possibility.

Let me give you some help. Use this chapter's pointer like a new pair of jeans. Try on some new jeans. See how they fit. In fact, wear them out and about and see how they feel in your day-to-day world. What is the beauty of a new pair of jeans? If you don't like them, you can simply grab the old pair and go back to wearing them. Think about this for a minute. See the world in a new way knowing that there has been nothing taken away from you. A new notion will not stop you from both holding the old one in abeyance and reinserting it if you wish. Wow, there is no threat in new possibilities! Why, then, do we act like there is? I suspect that in our conditioning we have been taught that new stories can lead us astray. In this way, we believe we are a culture with less religion than ever before, but we insist on holding our non-religious beliefs in the same way religious zealots all understand. Yep, you got it. Religious insecurity is in your mothers' milk and we practice it steadfastly in our so-called secular world. Awakening is not a religious event. Rather it is an event in consciousness.

I really cannot leave you with just one Nasruddin story. Here is another. One day a friend of Nasiruddin's named Mahmood approaches him with a proposition. "Nasruddin, have I got a bargain for you! An elephant! A real, life-sized living elephant! And for just one thousand rupees."

Nasruddin replies, "Are you nuts? What do I want with an elephant?"

"It's a beautiful elephant. All gray. Ten feet tall with a complete trunk", replies Mahmood.

"But I have nothing to feed it. I have no place to put it. I live in a three-bedroom apartment!"

"But, Nasruddin, two beautiful tusks maybe two feet long each. It is a magnificent animal. They don't make them like this anymore."

"Mahmood!" Nasruddin yells at the top of his lungs, "I have a three-room walkup apartment on the sixth floor. Where will I keep an elephant?"

Mahmood, exasperated, replies, "You are a hard man, Nasruddin. I tell you what. I will throw in a second whole elephant for only a hundred rupees extra." At that Nasruddin replies, "Now, you're talking."

The art of the deal makes so many captive to its wiles. The activity of buying is so ingrained that even our own argument of not needing something does not reach our own core. In the end, our unconscious behavior overtakes our ability to do something that is obvious. Here is my advice. Treat all of it like a new pair of jeans. Take this pointer and this new approach. You can always go back to Mahmood as he will, I am sure, have a couple of elephants for you and you can carry on, like you always have!

part three

——•○ ⊱◦⊰ ○•——

Looking Under the Hood

chapter fifteen

———•◦ ⚬◦•———

cognition and story

S OME YEARS BACK, Ramesh Balsekar was visited by a Buddhist monk. The monk asked how someone could become enlightened. Ramesh responded, "Who is this one that wants to become enlightened?"

The monk responded, "From a Buddhist point of view I would say that this 'one' is nothing more than a bundle of consciousness, concepts, ideas, feelings and experiences."

Ramesh immediately responded, "So are we random pieces of this laundry list of stuff or are we an amalgamation or entity?"

The monk sat puzzled for a second and then countered, "I know that when I speak of one that wants to become enlightened, I am holding it as one thing. Yet at the same time, I know that one thing is but a variety of what I mentioned. How do we cross this line from lots of particulars to one thing?"

Ramesh immediately responded, "Cognition. It is the glue that creates the bundling of which you speak. Think about it and you will see that we assign certain particulars to each body mind to produce a theme, as it were. In order to do that, we actually predict that what we have seen will occur again. We make a random happening a predicted feature. If someone is angry then that becomes a part of how we construct their theme. But can't anger simply appear sometimes and not others?"

The monk then lit up, "This is the part that has always bothered me. If something different than what we expect happens then we have to change or update our theme. Why can't we hold that a person is an unexpected producer of whatever comes?"

Ramesh, with a smirk, said, "Because there wouldn't be one that could be enlightened if there wasn't a container for all of these happenings, which we now call characteristics, as though we knew they belonged to one entity. We cognize the created summary of each so-called individual and treat them as though it were so." Why the smirk? Ramesh knew that first we make up the one to be enlightened. Then we assume it into story existence and ask questions about it. How often is life rendered in stories that need empty assumptions to prop them up? Cognition is a strong glue even when holding nothing together!

It is in this exchange that you will find the one little piece that detours all of us into a false identification. Cognition. Do you see it? It is the notion of bundling. Do "you" come bundled or do you have to process all of the particulars of "you" to construct or bundle something? You know that when we speak of each other, we do so in a bundled form. What is happening out there in pieces and parts has been processed into "one" thing. This is really important as it is the conflation that has us believe we come bundled. We do not. We create that in our cognition-story continuum. That is to say, we intellectually produce who we are.

Think about the words in the response to the Buddhist monk. What pieces are always present in raw form? What pieces are not? Consciousness is the only direct occurrence in manifestation in the definition of an "I". What about bundles, concepts, and ideas? All of those are processed.

The monk used the term bundled. How does this bundling happen? And what is the result of that bundling? Why is this so important? Anything that is bundled is simply a result that is manufactured for one reason and one reason only. It is done to hold a spot in your mind. It does not actually live out there, as there are only bits and pieces standing on their own with no meaning. They simply exist in consciousness. We have to create in order to get the rest. Can you see that story is the same thing? It is a product. In all of my time with Ramesh he spent the majority of his time teasing this little difference out. There is no "I" other than your creation of it. What you really are is beyond the processed concept or story. When I speak of conflation, this is what I am pointing to. When you call yourself "I" you think you are saying something that relates to manifestation. You really aren't.

CHILD STORY

Guess what, you are a story in the common holding. Not only are you *in* a story, it turns out that you *are* the story. Child development experts often claim that until about the age of two a growing infant does not distinguish between himself and his mother. In fact, he does not distinguish between himself and the entirety of the rest of the world. The very first learning that a child develops is the assumption that he is autonomous and separate from the rest of the world. That learning is one of the basic building blocks of story. From that moment on, his entire world will feed and cultivate this worldview.

And what is the internal movement that takes a child from undifferentiated phenomena, of which he is a part, to an understanding that he is a separate actor moving through a terrain of manifestation? Actually, it is quite simple. Because this is the first building block of story development, it is also the first activity of intellect that a so-called separate being undertakes. The extraction of some phenomena, from the entirety that is available, is defined as cognition. How do we know what to extract and what to leave behind? Once again, we are taught which things are important and which things are not. Cognition includes as its main driver the element of meaning making. In other words, once a piece of content can be contrasted with another piece, the opportunity for extraction is available. And which pieces should be extracted depend on the context, culture, family, religion and so forth into which a child has been placed in order to move through this piece of development.

What Is Important In Your Story?

Yep. There are two stories here. You as a body-mind, indeed, are the machine that through your intellect renders one thing and discards another to create the story you live within. But there is also the story of the machine itself. You walk, talk, and engage, leaving an identifiable trail of story bits behind you. Hence, we have the story of the story-making machine.

Cognition, then, is simply the active story creation utilizing elements embedded in the intellect in order to make sense of an otherwise overwhelming and undifferentiated world. Is there an absolute within this undifferentiated content that all people recognize? If there is, we certainly have never come to any agreement in all of our history. For it is this basic lack of agreement, along with the insistence that our story making is real, that gives rise to all activities within the human domain. In this regard there is little difference between the Civil War and a beautiful wedding.

Cognition operates on what humans view as an arc. All cultures have a mainstream movement of ideas and concepts woven into their very construction. In first grade we learn addition, in second grade we learn subtraction, and by fourth grade we are experts at multiplication. The faculty of cognition is operable at every level by extracting what is deemed to be recognizable and rendering it into a further recognizable item. Because of this assumed arc of sophistication and maturity, humans within their integrated groups hold unconscious agreement as to what is highest or lowest on the arc of development. It is very important to understand this.

Ranking is Cognition in Action

One of the prejudices of cognition that seemingly appears in all cultures and societies is that theories, models and systems are all a higher form of intellectual achievement than is the simple story. Thus, a small child can lose herself in the enchantments of a fairy kingdom, and this is deemed to be early developmental behavior. Meanwhile, the nuclear scientist can lose himself in string theory and this is deemed to be later developmental behavior. But the reality is that cognition itself starts at story making. And it is at this level that string theory, financial business cases and the like all begin. In fact, it could be said that the earlier cognitive operation holds more essence than most anything that follows. What do I mean by this? When the most intricate and sophisticated models are reduced into a story that you can understand it becomes vibrant and even emotional. The reality is that story has the possibility of holding much more of the initial elements of undifferentiated consciousness than the distant models worshiped by developed adults everywhere.

Some years ago, a gathering of scientists in Kona, Hawaii took place. It seems that they were harvesting data as to the origin of the moon. They knew that all of the stories of the moon's emergence were being proven dead wrong by the data that they were collecting. And there came a moment where they realized that they had to gather and create the story that the data would explain. For with no story, they had nothing that could be rendered or delivered in order for other story-based humans to onboard or cognize. You see, we have become so accomplished at accumulating pieces without knowing the story, that this collection effort called science, itself, has become a story. Nevertheless, we are convinced that understanding graphs and spreadsheets are of some higher order. Our science is based on a collective standing around muttering to themselves, "Wow, it has numbers, data, it must be higher order stuff!"

STORY POINTERS ARE A RECLAIMING OF ESSENCE

Story pointers have as essence the return to the place that holds your authenticity. Where would that likely be? It would be the place that has the potential to hold the tangible and emotional sense that is the center of your very reality. Story pointers hold that the earliest story cognized by you has that potential. I often refer to that place as original myth, your original myth. For most, in order to return to that most powerful of places requires the dropping of a lifetime judgment that story is a lesser version of where they might already stand. In fact, most compelling stories simply do not require the intellectual add-ons accumulated in most adults' lifetimes. Let me stop here for just a second to point out one thing. Ultimately your story, like all stories, is simply a concept that has no reality except its appearance in consciousness itself. It only arises in the cognized output of the intellect. So, in this story exercise, we let the story stand as though it were real and dig to the bottom. Once we have arrived, we can move to the misidentification stage. It is all in the seeking!

The fact of the matter is that in order to begin your trek into story pointers you must be available to try on a few of the attributes of story. The first is that you are in a story and in fact you are a story yourself. The second is to recognize that the first behavior that you learned is cognition. Cognition is simply the rendering of unwieldy and overwhelming content into a consensus version of meaning. It is such an old behavior that it long ago became automatic and unconscious. A large part of story pointers is becoming aware of what has been long lost in order to move closer to our own original authenticity. It is the conscious carrying of your own original authenticity that is the power behind this personal life process. It is always happening. The question is whether you are anywhere within its movement.

Pointers to awakening live in a much different way than concepts that claim to be true. They are tangible and compelling all at the same time. When dissected in intellectual writing, inevitably these become two and are considered in separate pieces. In this case the writer imagines "tangible and compelling" separately. Then they are teased out and dealt with piece by piece. All concepts are built the same way. But no amount of effort can put Humpty Dumpty back together again. Nonetheless, we are conditioned to search for some truth in all we onboard. We rarely, if ever, stop to think, "Is there such a thing as truth in what I extract from all that is?" In the world of sages and pointers it is often said that you and I are concepts. I personally do not like that languaging. It makes it difficult to imagine you and I as robust tangible objects in space and time. Rather, it leads the typical seeker to hold himself the same way as some typical washed-out paragraph in a second-rate novel.

YOU ARE THE STORY ITSELF

I want to repeat some important basics for you at this point. We all have lived a life replete with story. As a child it likely was not unusual to read, embrace and occupy the enchanted kingdom of fairy tales and other children's stories. We know the story territory to be one of compelling imagination and tangibility at the same time. In fact, we lived it in our child minds as though there were no difference between that journey and a walk down the obvious "real" street outside. But as we age, we relegate that experience to childhood and become educated adults. We now know that flights of childhood fancy rank several levels below real life. And by organizing our frame of reference in that way we marginalize our greatest asset on the spiritual journey and replace it with the dull, dusty building blocks of intellectual construction. Our marginalization is so complete that the best possibility we allow ourselves is that of a storyteller.

Adults, you see, must stand on the outside of the story itself and rise only to the place of its teller. We have banished ourselves from being the story itself, yet this placement is exactly what a pointer invites. You and the story you cognize always arise together. In fact, it is only in intellect that we can separate these into two things, one of which we simply ignore.

It was commonplace in my time with Ramesh Balsekar to hear him tell seekers on the path, "When you consider consciousness do not place yourself on the outside as an observer. You are part of all that arises and live as consciousness yourself". My version would be to say, "You are the story itself. You do yourself no service placing yourself as a concept-observer of an arising story and assigning yourself to the paltry position of its teller."

STORY AND COGNITION ARE NOT TWO THINGS

I would be so bold as to submit that cognition itself is exclusively extended and rendered as story. Here you can see that both of these so-called concepts must be considered a single unit. Where else have we seen this type of combining in order to deliver a breakthrough understanding? Look no further than Einstein and his framing of time and space. He insisted that these supposed two concepts were a single thing commonly referred to as a space-time continuum. The extension of time allowed space to be and conversely the extension of space allowed time to be. They simply could not be considered separately and to do so was to create a story "as if" one could. Cognition and story are of exactly the same ilk. The extension of cognition allows story to be, and the extension of story allows cognition to be. Why am I so insistent that story is the inextricable companion to cognition and vice versa? The always and natural rendering of all cognition is in story.

As a seeker, begin to allow yourself to understand that you are the story itself. There is no outside in which to stand and observe. You do it anyway, but that supposed action is contrived, and you have likely created an unconscious story "as if" you could stand out there. That contrived separation simply does not exist other than in your intellectual insistence that it be the case. When you cognize, you are simply rendering a story. You are the cognition and the story arising all at once. Let's be bold and act like Einstein and declare the processing of consciousness as "you" to be the story-cognition continuum. Wow, this is an exciting moment!

LINGUISTIC IMPRINTING

As a result of living in an assumptive state, which includes a daily life in which each body and mind are considered an independent autonomous entity, we have conveniently assembled a societal system to incessantly imprint on ourselves that this is the case. We assume that you and I are different things. Therefore, it must be necessary, that when there are two things, that communication between the two must be carried on. As a result, language is needed for these obviously separate entities to speak to one another. The interesting thing about language is that it lives in the emotional field nested in consciousness itself. That is to say, that when expressed, language holds tangibility in the conscious field within which we live.

Because we live in duality, which allows our intellect to identify contrast, we can assumptively hold individuation as an object in the field of our conscious experience. Of course, our language and every other format and conscious constellation are rendered into similar subject-object formulations. I am the subject and all else is the object or are the objects. Because of the tangibility of lived experience, which includes language itself, we are in a process of constantly confirming, to the so-called other, that we are indeed separate entities. And, in our infinite wisdom, we have additionally decided that each of these entities has volition in and of themselves. These stories that are carried by the tangibility of our language are in a continual process of hammering the assumptive point of separation into our similarly assumed separate selves. This process is called conditioning or imprinting. Human body-minds live in an ever-present alive platform of contrast and separation. The ego itself is nothing more than a concept, the principal concept, of this exercise. Every time I address you as "you" or you address me as "me" we are executing on our assumption that we are indeed separate things. Because this address is tangible and in the field of consciousness, it delivers a felt experience that this is the case.

So, linguistic imprinting is the component of language that we use with one another in an avalanche of daily communication. This is the quintessential "As If" example. We act as if we know we are separate, including rendering the entirety of who we are into separate pieces. Even this writing, as you read it, implies that some separate object is communicating to you, another separate object, a body of content. But is that what is happening?

Some weeks back I was involved in a discussion with a fairly well-known biological scientist. As you might expect, he was very clear about the fact that phenomena subject to scientific testing was clearly true in a way that other concepts were not. My response was that if life were a game and we had indeed created both the board and all the pieces that moved on the board, that the game would result in exactly the way we had designed it. And if we agreed that we were indeed separate beings, even though no definition of a separate being could ever be crystallized, then, of course, we could test the phenomenon that accompanied that assumption. But, ultimately, science itself was a part of the game and was testing the assumptions that comprise the game itself.

As we moved through this discussion this brilliant man made the following comment. "Alan, I see exactly what you're pointing at. And if we simply hold that our assumptions are an empty set awaiting a possibility of consciousness to point to its larger story, then there really isn't anything to talk about."

My response. "Exactly".

YOU MEAN WE ALREADY KNOW THIS?

Yes, yes, we do. It is common to hear the term confirmation bias or cognitive bias. There are dozens of related terms in the field of learning and individual psychology. In fact, I recently saw a meme that listed 50 versions of such bias. The suggestion was that we should all memorize them as though that might help. But isn't the ego memorizing something still imbedded in its cognitive patterning? You know the answer. Humanity both knows and has developed such concepts. We know. But then what do we do? We blithely move along after learning such things and pretend to one and all that there is no such bias in our day-to-day movements. When was the last time someone explained to you that all that they delivered was essentially bent by the frames they carried in their story making? They could then go on and explain that all concepts living in separation yielded faulty perception. What about concepts of non-separation? There aren't any. That is why we use pointers to attempt to induce a perception that is not egoic. Can that be reduced to a non-dual concept? Why, no it can't. You see all of this story and cognition exposition is imbedded in the separative nature of all duality.

alan e. shelton

THE STORY THAT DOESN'T ASSUME SEPARATION

Consciousness reveals itself to itself in duality. Remember Einstein's space-time continuum? That continuum allows for the arising of identifiable content to occur. No space and no time yields no appearance of anything. The human body-mind appears within this continuum and uses cognition and story as another continuum in order to render the sense on being within the space-time container. When one assumes that each body-mind is a particular and separate entity, then the story that is cognized is often referred to as the small story. That is to say, the intellect has the capability to organize a story for each separate body-mind and all the objects and particulars required. This results in a complete story. However, when consciousness is cognized in a single non-duality arising within all that is, this is referred to as the big story.

Awakening is a happening within phenomenality. All happenings are held in memory as stories. Awakening is simply the larger version in which contrast is not rendered into meaning. Meaning making is an act of separation which cannot but create conflict and a lack of peace. The place of permanent peace is located phenomenally in the larger and deeper story of consciousness itself. Because this is the case, it must be seen that one is continually subject to a meaning making process. This process is called conditioning, and it cements in place a story that cannot lead to awakening.

Pointers are a doorway to a stance in a place of awareness. In that place, all that arises is within the consciousness

219

of non-duality. Often the question that is asked is, "Who is aware of the story?" This question is a tangible and energetic call, formed linguistically in the emotional field of consciousness, which points to another story that is commonly referred to as awakening. This pointer is simply the noticing of the ongoing ego imprinting of conditioning. The obvious question then is, "Who is aware of this ongoing imprinting?" You intuitively know that there is a vantage point from which all that occurs within the so-called happening of our individual stories can be seen. It is that awareness that you ultimately are. And the question is designed to hold the tangibility that will point you to a standing within phenomenality, in which you will recognize yourself.

As you go through your daily routine, notice how individuals spend the majority of their time establishing exactly who they are as separate entities. Even in relationships that have lasted for decades, the participants spend endless conversations in describing to their significant other who they really are. One would think that after living with someone for years that such an explanation would not be necessary. And in fact, it is not. This conversation is simply the self-talk in which the ego must participate in order to continuously assure itself that it is indeed a separate, autonomous decision-maker. For it intuitively knows that at some deep level, within the larger story, that this is not the case. But the ego, being the ego, is dead set on making this a reality no matter the invitation to the contrary. And, as a result, you and I live in a world where we actually believe that there is a 'you' and 'I' in more than an empty set. But if we know that such is the case, and all pointers are an invitation to that knowing, who is aware that this is so?

And let's not forget causality as one of the culprits in maintaining our separate entity point of view. To whom or what does causality happen? It happens to extractions only. One thing cognitively extracted appears to impact or cause a happening to another cognized object. Much like the example of language above, the continuous cognition within duality creates dualism. Dualism is the belief that all happenings are post cognitive. Uh oh! That eliminates the entire journey from the end of cognition to the prior unity that birthed it. I often tell folks that seeing all that is as an arising, with no prior cause and no impact on subsequent objects, is a way to interrupt the incessant cognitive pattern. Will the mind pay any attention to that? No, it will not. But the living understanding of non-causative arising can resonate with consciousness itself. See the imprinting of your story identity as the ongoing rat-a-tat that it is. Causation, language, bundling, conflation; all are holding hands in the production of your autonomous assumption of life with you as the outside observer.

THE STORY CONFLATION

Remember that we covered the conflation of consciousness and story? How does that happen? As consciousnesses absent cognition, we are an indefinable essence. I often say that we simply know that we exist, or that existence is the felt sense of consciousness. The rest is interpretation. All of that interpretation is the product of cognition within the assumptive state of separation and in time and space. We attach the raw and undefined sense of existence to ourselves. That simply results in our paltry ego story being embedded with our very sense of existence. We call that our story self or identity. Then we take that small ego object as who we are, rather than the sense of existence itself. We conflate the two things. Awakening is simply the perception from the pure awareness that you are with the rest of the miscellaneous objects of consciousness arising within. You will no longer conflate the two things, nor will you ever be fooled again.

So here is the takeaway. You are equipped with the capability within your mind/body to extract bits and pieces of manifestation. You then manufacture that extraction into a construction or bundling, as our monk would say. That is cognition and story creation that lives in a single process. If that is all that you think you are then you will believe your living is happening within that extraction of separation. What separation? The one that appears to be the case due to our facility in intellect to make it so.

The spiritual trek is nothing more that the inquiry, "What was I before cognition?" Why is this inquiry important? Because we intuitively know that when we live in separation, we feel that something is amiss. What is amiss? We have left the directly perceived world of "all that is" behind, as though it never was. Being, also known as presence, cannot be captured in intellect. It lives in the ineffability of prior unity, the unity in which there is no construction. Do we lose the bundling activity within ourselves upon awakening? No, we do not. We simply open up the birthright of ours that we seemingly lost because we bought into an idea that it does not exist.

chapter sixteen

—•◦ ⚙ ◦•—

Automatic Behavior

HUMANS HAVE DEDUCED who they are and how they function. It is an assumption to be sure. In fact, most knowledge-based writings are an ongoing argument of replacing pieces of the human assumption with other, supposedly more evolved, pieces of intellectual concept. So, what is this assumption? Mankind assumes that it is composed of independent decision-making units or entities. Each of these entities is indeed seen as the author of its own journey in life. Why do we assume such? It turns out that, like other sentient beings, we occupy a body form. It is easy to assume that body roughly equivalates to a separate entity. From our earliest memory we have been in extensive immersion into this assumption. Families, tribes, schools, and religions all subscribe to this assumption. So much so that they have indeed forgot it was an assumption. We have now entered into the realm of automatic behavior.

The body-mind, along with the energetic you, comes with amazing options. It's as if we went to the body-mind dealer and picked them out. When we did, we all selected the store and execute option known as automatic behavior.

Why did we do that? Well, it turns out that the brain can only pay attention to one thing at a time in a present way. So, it became necessary to find a way that learnings from prior experience could still be in play so we could function in a way we all call human.

Let me give you an example. We likely all remember when we learned to drive. I am from California, so driving is a badge of the story of my heritage. If you are at all like me, you cannot help but remember the experience of learning to drive. Even if you went to the oft required driver training and education, the actual experiential encounter with the process was overwhelming. First of all, there were the things in the car itself. The steering wheel, brakes, seat belts. mirrors, transmission, foot pedals, turn signals and on and on. It seemed literally impossible to remember, let alone use all of these doodads. On top of that, there were the rules of the road along with signs, lines painted in the street, lights, curbs, no curbs and on and on. Now, add to that knowing how to execute driving with touch and feel and you have a real myriad of stuff to track.

You may think back to that time and recall that you had to focus and think even to get part of the experience handled. What was happening here? Whenever we are learning something new we use our attention or awareness, which at the learning stage has to hold all of the pieces of any undertaking. Do you remember how awkward it was? You had to think of every item. Put the car in gear then use the gas pedal or brake. Then look at a sign or in the rear-view mirror. Do you recall how it felt that it was impossible to do all that at the speed that driving seemed to require? It felt too packed and overwhelming. I vividly can still see the thoughts racing across my mind asking how this was even possible. And then I would watch others drive and feel I would never be able to do what was happening in front of my eyes. But then something magical happened. In a scant few weeks, we would cruise into the garage, flip up the garage door, throw the keys in the car, put it into gear and bang out on to the road. All of that overwhelm was gone. Tracking all of the endless parts of the experience did not need to happen. We just did it without the thinking piece which was so difficult. This is a great example of automatic behavior.

But what happened? The ability of the human brain seems to locate in two phases. The first is the simple attention or awareness of right now. If you used a computer analogy, we would call this ROM. Random Operating Memory is that which is used for the task at hand. Then there is RAM, which is Random Access Memory, which holds things that can be recalled at any time. As humans we seem to have a RAM box called automatic behavior. All of the things that are needed but no longer in your awareness sit available for use. In the human version these things are connected to a catalyst or trigger. When you drive your car the automatic behavior box reacts based on the input it has already classified and stored away. This is a beautiful and efficient function that allows the human body-mind to extend itself much further than we might expect. That is the good news. However, this feature of our behavior comes with a downside. The behavior that is stored, or automatic behavior, is created to meet a certain story. The driving example is a good one. How you drive at the time you learn is the story that the automatic behavior box utilizes. Once the behavior is stored the story itself disappears and becomes long forgotten. The other feature is that the behavior is trigger actuated. The mind knows immediately how to behave based on the trigger or catalyst it recognizes.

One of my favorite movies is an old one from the 80's called *Starman*. Jeff Bridges portrays an alien who, along with his co-star Karen Allen, is attempting to be picked up by his alien space tribe which will be landing a craft in Nevada somewhere. In order to get there a long drive in a car must be made. Now, Jeff's alien character must have an automatic behavior box as well. It seems that he simply absorbs whatever he sees as behavior and then replicates it on demand. Of course, he simply onboards the driving style of Karen Allen which would make one think all would go well. It turns out that his driving teacher can be aggressive especially on yellow lights. In fact, the Jeff character stores that yellow lights must mean that one should slam the gas pedal to the floor and go like hell. When Jeff takes the wheel, he employs this at a light where there is a large semi-truck loaded down with hay creating a large crash and putting them in danger. The conversation between the two as they barely escape death goes something like this:

"I thought you watched me and knew the rules."
"I did watch you and I do know the rules".
"But you almost got us killed."

"The rules are red light stop, green light go, yellow light go very fast".

What is that? You got it. Automatic behavior.

This process, while creating great reach for the equipment the body-mind possesses, is entirely reactive. That is to say, when the trigger is recognized the automatic behavior engages with no story to check and see if it is the proper behavior. Remember that story checking is in the ROM box of being present but carries with it the cumbersome corollary of slowness in efficient living. However, we are taught to live efficiently and move most everything we can unconsciously into the RAM box. Why does this matter? All of your assumptive states are held within this box. The fact of the matter is that most of our stories are not based in anything other than belief. We believe the world is a certain way and we act "as if" that were the case. This "as if" now becomes unconscious because behavior is simply generated based on a trigger with no story present. In other words, we act most of the time reactively.

I love dogs. In my later life I have had the privilege of being able to adopt several rescued dogs. I love these guys. That said, rescued dogs come with their automatic behavior already installed. Many times, these behaviors are responses to abuse they may have suffered in their earlier life. Now, there is no doubt that when they are in my care that they have nothing to worry about. I know this and they seem to know that as well. But I always have to watch and see how they react to different movements of mine, as they will react. They have triggers which activate the behaviors they have stored in their canine intellect. Over time they may adjust but some are so indelible that no adjustment ever happens. I love this mirror of how sentience is built. You and I are the same. We have a trigger that throws us into so-called independent behavior. Is there such a thing? We likely have never asked that question.

This brings us back to what we assume we, ourselves, are. We have learned that we are an autonomous author of our very own existence. This is coupled with the notion that we are separate from all else in existence. Of course, since human need as taught in the knowledge path demands that we be right, guess what? We accept all information that supports our assumptions and reject all that does not. Remember confirmation bias? Now you might begin to see why there is a seekers hole and how difficult it is to understand how to get out. The seeking journey is one of dissolving assumptions and not replacing them. Why? Because your true identity is one that lives here and now and is not an intellectual concept. The dissolving is intended to drop the bottom out of your automatic behavior and deliver you into your true story. That story has no intellectual basis and exists much differently than you might imagine.

MARKERS AND DISTINCTIONS

So, what is a way to deal with automatic behavior as you tease it out of your assumptive life? Markers and distinctions are a simple way to engage with outside manifestation in a disciplined way. It is a pointer. Yes, it is a concept and, as Ramana would say, a thorn. In other words, we carry an assumption that we do not see. A pointer is introduced to help see that our assumption is an obstacle to our own natural authenticity. Of course, once we employ such a device and it dissolves the originally held concept, it becomes unnecessary. So, if you have no use for this pointer or use it until it has no effect then simply throw it away as you would any thorn you use to dig out an imbedded thorn. Sometimes, though, it helps to have a step in between.

Then what is the assumption we are dealing with here? Many times, upon hearing a pointer, folks talk about how we should never forget to honor the relative or individual within us. Why is that? It is because most pointers usher you, the seeker, towards seeing that our relative or individual self as we construct it, creates the bondage we are attempting to escape. What we do not see is our unbridled worship of this individual self and our stubborn insistence on tethering all of our cognition to this separate notion.

In that egoic assumption the individual is a defined object navigating a world of manifestation to which she must attach meaning, continuing the separation of herself from all else. When a notion that "all arises together" is introduced we attempt to combat such a notion with our continued meaning making, which is useless in a non-bound-aried arising. We are addicted to meaning making to such an extent that we slip consistently into creating meaning making pieces even when we claim we are embracing all that is. This pointer is simply a way to notice when that slippage is occurring or has occurred.

I find that the search for awakening is much the same as the bicycle story. The addiction to manifestation or "what is out there" is so strong that all solutions include meaning making from pieces and parts that already are much too emphasized. So, how do we find balance? The addiction to meaning making blocks out the possibility of standing in awareness, as it were. Much like our bicycle story, our world is lying on its left side and "lean to the left" is what we teach.

As consciousness we are a fascinating combination of the detail in motion of manifestation and the stillness in presence of witnessing. To that we have added the notion that each body-mind is an autonomous decision maker and labeled that decider the ego. That addition has become the entire concept of self while obscuring or abandoning the witness nature of who we are. All pointers are aimed at finding the balance of the duality that makes us "us". And when a perception is so unbalanced as to entirely block out an aspect, the pointer will point one at the unseen part that the assumptive state of our living hides.

We worship manifestation, or the moving parts aspect, of our perception. We ignore the witness that we are or simply do not know it is there. This pointer is to underscore our witness nature and notice when we unknowingly slip away from it.

A marker is simply the line between manifestation and your sense of existence. When you locate and abide in your sense of existence, many times you will unwittingly slip into your normal meaning-making mode of cognition, thinking you are still in your witness. Notice when this happens and begin to note what the difference is between the two. As you do this you are creating for yourself a distinction. The marker tells you that the movement has occurred. The distinction tells you from where you have moved.

Now I know that you have heard that there is no watcher or nothing to be watched. This is true. But that will not be seen until the identification you have with your ego-self drops. Until then the world comes in parts. Establish yourself in the witness until the day comes that there are no markers and distinctions. That will be the day that both thorns are removed. Until then, use your awareness of being out of balance to cease to occupy the identified place of "me".

There is one marker and its distinction, one only, that a seeker actually needs. It is the same as the famous comment by Nisargadatta. To paraphrase, "My master told me to pay attention to the "I Am" and that is all I did". Yep, he tilted his bike to the left! To be a seeker one must be prepared to scrap the entirety of everything that has led to now. This includes the so-called absolute surety that manifestation is meaningful and should be constantly scoured for its meaning. The one marker is to note when one is looking out for meaning and when one is abiding in the witness meaning-free. Then, like Nisargadatta, install yourself in the witness and forget tracking the outside world for its meaning. Know the distinction between the outside and the inside and pay attention to the marker that tells you when the boundary has been crossed.

Upon hearing this you may, like many seekers, begin to defend the need of the relative manifestation where all is cognized into pieces. "It's what we are as humans" or "It's the dignity that we are" and other dribble. Trust me, the world of separation has no need for defending. All your defending is really your reticence to scrap what you are sure is true. There is no truth, only consciousness, which has no separate pieces to declare as truthful. A distinction, as ferreted out by a marker, is an exercise in separation until it collapses and then it is no longer seen in separation.

As I tell many of my questioners, see that it is part of our stubborn insistence to call out how consciousness itself should act. If that stubbornness is your pointer, go get a latte and quit seeking. You will be happier.

TETHER YOUR CAMEL

Guess what? Many seekers are the exact opposite of the ones that seem insulted that relative or separated experience gets little positive notice in non-dual writing. Of course! Now these folks want to ignore the relative world and pretend that the only place to live is in the so-called spiritual only. This is commonly called bypassing as though we get to ignore all others and their predicaments. Not only do we get to engage in this bypassing, we do it with the seal of approval of non-dual teachings and pointers. Okay, so let's do a lean to the right pointer and call it *Tether Your Camel*. There is an old famous Sufi saying that goes like this. "Praise God, but don't forget to tether your camel". Always remember that if you can lean too far to the left, you can also lean too far to the right. Pointers are not for creating a refuge for seekers to attach themselves and quote crap to the rest of the spiritual world. Yes, I know that is a frequent happening by simply reading the scores of folks who do exactly that. A marker is simply a part of a pointer. It is a bit like a turn signal on a car. You see the signal and know a car is attached. Don't use a pointer to "Bible bash". Simply see it and let it point. Don't be like the "sour grapes" folks who claim that awakening simply isn't possible because they can't argue it out. Story identities are scattered throughout our spiritual world proclaiming this and that as though egos embracing illusionary truth is a path of some kind. Get used to the noise and don't let it distract you from your own journey.

chapter seventeen

——•◦ ⚬◉⚬ ◦•——

Taking Delivery and the Need to Feed

S OMETIMES POINTERS are so intertwined that
they need to be exposed together. So, let's review a bit
here in order to get to the meat. We believe we are the stories that are created in our minds as a part of the process
of being conditioned in our context. That context includes
family, society, schooling and media. In other words, the
assault on our cognitive facilities is so overwhelming that
the story of our entification, that we are separate and autonomous authors of our own journey, is imbedded as a
default. If we were a computer program, which the body
mind might resemble, the program downloaded includes
this as a default preference or setting. We then live "as if"
this default were the case.

This basic default feeds into many dependent story behaviors. How could it be otherwise? First, we identify with
our sense of separation. Then, that very frame is applied
to all of the rest of our activity. The ego is simply a story of
separation to which consciousness has glued itself to pro-

vide the constant feedback that our default assumption is in play.

Taking delivery is simply a pointer that moves your awareness back into the process as it happened before a story assumption is loaded into automatic behavior. Before one stores content for automatic behavior, that perceptive input is claimed as "mine". This claiming is called taking delivery. Why do we call it that? As long as you believe and act as if you are the ego, anything that comes in upon which you act must be received as property of the ego, as it were. There is a taking delivery happening here by the ego. This happens initially, as I said, in the awareness of here and now.

Now, it has likely been so long since that taking delivery was conscious or noticed that it now happens automatically. This pointer seeks to have you notice that when in the throes of response to the delivery that there must have been a point the delivery was accepted. The possibility of this pointer is that you will come to a place where you see something that your ego would normally claim before that claiming takes place. From where do we see this ego claiming? We see it from outside the ego. We then can begin to understand what wants to happen as some ego deliveries are not ours and others are. We open ourselves to the possibility that we will simply be lived rather than jumping on all input like a live grenade.

In the beginning, you notice you are well into response before you think of wanting to be there at the delivery moment. That is OK. Keep asking when the delivery happened. You will notice that it comes earlier and earlier until you see it upon its first moment. This is not to encourage you to be in a place where "you" make an earlier decision. But rather you will notice that seeing the event at inception will yield that some of them are received and others not. And all of that will happen without your supposed autonomous self being involved. There is an old adage, "Not my Circus. Not my Monkeys". Taking delivery is the claiming of all monkeys as yours!

THE NEED TO FEED

A closely related pointer is one called the *Need to Feed*. This is the egoic assumption that there is something in our created stories called truth and that we are called as warriors to distill and protect such truths. Perhaps the best battlefield to see this in action is Facebook. Facebook claims to be a place for community to connect. But a two-minute visit will reveal that it seems to be a battlefield for the witty and barbed argument to have its day. There is a string of call and responses contained within a display called a thread. This thread seems to be an exercise in pelting various entrants in the thread with both personal and so-called facts until in the end a victory can be claimed.

You all know that these so-called parts and pieces are but a story cobbled together in the mind of the combatants. Did you ever get into one of these discussions and you can't help but get back into the fray? That last comment is one that has to be answered. That need to respond dominates your mind until the response is delivered and there is a moment where you think you have said something. Not only have you said something, but it is likely the most well written and cogent argument ever delivered in the history of human thought. Well, if you have lived such a drama then you have been ensconced in the need to feed. Who is the "you"? Why it is your ego attempting to prove that it not only is something but that it's necessary to your very existence. How does it prove that? It does so by being the most equipped warrior of truth ever found. Think a minute about truth. Who needs it? Your ego does. Without truth what would the ego fight for? It turns out that the need to feed relies on taking delivery. Take delivery and fight to the rhetorical death. Remember that all contrast must live in tension to even exist. What could be a more tension laden experience than the need to feed? The relaxation of getting outside of this activity is enough to begin the unraveling of the knot that is your ego and its concepts.

chapter eighteen

---

i can't breathe

DURING MY YEARS IN Peru, India, and the business world I was given the delicious opportunity to live and participate in the oral tradition. The teller, sometimes a guru, sometimes a CEO, and often a beggar, all deliver stories in the oral tradition and each is customized for the exact moment of telling. One of my favorite stories is attributed to the Zen tradition and uses the stereotype of the wise, Asian master with the girth of an elephant, "The Large Size Master." One can almost imagine a life-sized elephant in meditation. Here goes:

It seems that a disciple and acolyte of the fat elephant sized Zen master had worked for years to become enlightened. But, like many of us, his stubbornness in clinging had always exceeded his earnestness to understand. The normal approach for this master was to have his disciple lay next to him while he sat and gave wisdom. On this particular day as he discoursed, his disciple stopped him in mid-sentence with the plea, "Master, master, I can't breathe." In response, the master, in all his largesse, gathered himself up, only to immediately sit down on his disciple's chest. He looked deep into his eyes and demanded, "Breathe now, my beloved. Breathe now!"

Now most of us, in the masters' place, likely would have looked into our bag of knowledge and deduced that this was a medical emergency. And the normal emergency response would have occurred. But the master has another bag called wisdom. And when he looked into that bag, he found the cure for a spiritual emergency and proceeded to use it. It is amazing how well a human body can channel in air when a fat master is sitting on its chest! Why is this an important pointer?

Because we assume that we are each an independent decision-making unit defined approximately by the boundaries of our physical body. We respond to life as a series of issues to be resolved. In a nutshell, this is the position humanity always finds itself located. In today's world, we have wars, shootings, hate and violence. We consistently deem ourselves to be in a medical emergency, be it political, relationship or financial. What if the emergence of these events is simply consciousness sitting on our chest and pointing us to the inside? It does not have to be a fat Zen master. It could be any number of displays in consciousness that are deemed unfailingly to be problems but are not.

To change the reaction to such events is called the wisdom path. On the outside, all of our solutions are an exercise in separation attempting to cure separation. It has never worked and never will. And the onslaught continues. It is only in the non-separate essence of consciousness itself, that it can be seen that separation is a notion that really does not exist. This revelation is the only maturity that can ever arise in human affairs. But wait. Isn't earnestness the cornerstone to the spiritual journey. Isn't stubbornly making the same decision earnestness?

There is a difference between earnestness and stubbornness. Stubbornness is rooted in the ego and demands an attachment to some point of separation. Earnestness is the gift of consciousness that drives a seeker to find wisdom. One of my favorite metaphors is that of the Titanic. There is an old saying that warns us all not to engage in "rearranging the deck chairs on the Titanic" believing that this somehow will help the ship avoid its personal iceberg. Moving the deckchairs is a solution from the path of knowledge. We probably need to rearrange the deck chairs, so you have a different experience. What you get from this sort of problem-solving is a more organized seating chart for your boat. This will all make you feel better, until you hit the berg.

The path of knowledge, including furniture arranging, is the feeble attempt to egoically manage consciousness. It always looks out at the supposed separate pieces of manifestation, you know, the separate pieces called individuals. It believes that humans evolve, and things will get better. The path of wisdom always looks in. Evolution is irrelevant and the eternal moments of 'here and now' have neither color nor flavor. How could they? Consciousness is all that is. Consciousness does not evolve; it simply is. Intellectuals are wasting their time. Alligators are green and peacocks are blue. Both emerge from consciousness. What color is that? The same color as all the colors all at once. Nothing. No color at all. Now, the question for you is, "When will you breathe?" The master is sitting on your chest. Will you be one of the celebrated egos that try to fix separation on the outside or will you simply go inside and breathe? The air is inside.

THE WISDOM POND

When speaking about transformation and awakening there is one major thrust in all that can be said. We, as separate tangible egos, believe in an assumptive story demanding separateness. That demand leads to the further belief in a separate truth. Most of us spend much of our early life in our own version of activism that supports separate truth and separation. We argue, fight, and go to war all in the service of an assumption.

The path to awakening is an exercise in demolishing our own assumptive stories, which is all we have, and stepping into a new perception. This perception is often referred to as apperception or perception without a perceiver. Well that certainly takes care of our ego belief! We step from the world of autonomous doership with warriors and truth into the world of wisdom with consciousness as its only inhabitant.

In the ancient traditions, great warriors were taught to water the ground on which they performed their role.

This very knowing is indeed what made them a warrior. These warriors were encouraged to battle in order to leave behind a flourishing world for those they served. Why? Because being a warrior that simply fights ignores the wisdom of birthright to which all warriors are entitled. Warriors must know that warrior service is defined by its unwavering commitment to those served by the warrior activity. Otherwise, a warrior is reduced to a violent thug. Our current warrior class is a visible reminder of this.

In one small country long ago, the warriors would return from their toils and make their way to a hidden pond nearby the village. They commonly called this the Wisdom Pond. From their warrior's journey they would carry an old empty wooden bucket to be filled by the rickety old men at the pond. This bucket accompanied them on all of their activities. And at the end of their campaigns, they would freely water the field on which they had acted, giving it nourishment to bloom and transform. For the warrior's life includes the knowing to water the grounds that provide their very sustenance. But for all their might, they lacked the understanding of how to get the water from the pond and into the wooden buckets. For this they relied on the old men and women to whom the secrets of wisdom and water taking had been passed. These elders had once been warriors themselves and by luck lived to guard the old wisdom pond and lovingly handed water to all those warriors who could carry. This was the knowing of the old ones called sages.

And what did they have to learn to get water from the

pond? In reality, they had to unlearn. For it was only when they saw the water as the very same thing as themselves, did the water move freely into the buckets. And in so seeing they could not help but see that not just the water but also you, me and every other so-called object are simply consciousness. In fact, all there is, is consciousness.

For the majority of my life, I have been called to be a warrior. Yes, my mentors fashioned me to eventually become a wise man. But my focus was the daily grind, and I carried many a bucket back to the field of work like all the rest. The crowning moment in a long career was teaching story and leadership in the corporate world. This was a finishing for sure but still not yet the call to fill buckets. Finally, I had to ask, "What does it take to pull the water from the pond?"

It is the move from the story of separation into the story of non-duality or consciousness itself. But this is not just the movement within the intellect. It is the movement of identification. It is tangible in a way that thought simply isn't. We all identify or assertively live a story. The ego version starts at the notion that we are separate entities that author our own existence. It is the starting point of all beings with intellect. The non-dual version starts at the point that "all there is, is consciousness". All that arises within manifestation is emergent from the ground of "all that is". These two stories, warrior and sage, are lived in an energetic difference. One is duality with all of its pieces and parts being fashioned in some outcome. The other is a place of permanent peace. Awakening is simply the seeker's intuitive drive towards that peace. It is indeed the provenance of wisdom.

Wisdom is another activity, and yet non-activity entirely. Wisdom is the standing in the whole and seeing the individual emerge from consciousness. It is the location of identity in the whole and no longer in any one piece. This is the last bridge to cross in the development of consciousness itself and is often referred to as awakening.

I Often Say, "Saving the World is a Waste of Time Until you have Realized Yourself"

All acts in separation live in their dual nature. The so-called "saving the world" is developed from a prism of perception bent by separation. The solution is one of autonomous volition, which is nothing but the illusion of the intellect. Another illusion is the question of who thinks what in particular needs to be saved. Hunger, poverty and war are simply empty questions that draw separate egos to their support. Only when you realize that consciousness writes the script and you simply deliver the lines will your efforts be perfectly delivered. If you are meant to save the world then that will be your delivery on stage as you are lived into your original myth. But until you have realized yourself all will be a rendering of illusory choice, not the emergence of choiceless awareness.

chapter nineteen

———•◦ ⚬◦⚬ ◦•———

Diving to the Bottom

PERHAPS THE MOST challenging part of *Story Theory* is learning the sense of ongoing experiential tangibility. That is simply to say that the action is not in the intellectual and mental telling of the story but in the felt sense of the happening itself. For those of you who have ever attempted to change the nature of something you do physically, you will recognize this challenge. For instance, when a golfer needs to change the simple fundamental of how they grip the club, this challenge can feel monumental. By simply moving one's hands a few fractions of an inch from the original grip gives a swing an entirely new sense. And guess what? The human body, with full cooperation of the mind, will tend to move the grip back to its original place. While the mind knows that it wants to change the grip location, the body wants to follow the old story. That is why so many things we seek to change simply lapse back into the old habitual story. In order to actually make that change to the physical grip, an ongoing scanning system needs to be put in place to guarantee that change is possible. This is much like the journey within *Story Theory*.

So far, we have concentrated on shifting your felt experience from that of living in the map that you have previously assumed was experiential to change your grip on what you think is experience. In so doing, you can fully expect that you will have a tendency to move back into the conceptual realm of map living. The fact of the matter is that this kind of living is more comfortable, it is like the old golf grip. Many of the *Story Theory* terms are simply intended to operate as a scanning system to keep you in your newfound felt experience. Once you engage in a process of change you will always notice that the distinction between where you are coming from and where you are going to is fuzzy. That is because the clarity of where you are going to is not yet in your grasp. It still feels weird.

Due to the intellectual prowess of humanity, as expressed in science and technology, we are now comfortable with summarizing the experiential events of groups of humans as though that encapsulates experience itself. Peter Drucker, referred to often as the father of modern management, used to point out the difference between what folks held in their mental construction and what that very same concept would demand in existence to be real. One day I spun a story for him that made him chuckle. I told him the story about the gathering of all the bigtime nations currently called the G7. These largest seven economic powers in our world ostensibly gather to confront economic inequality in our global community.

Funny enough, they do so by analyzing sweeping and extracted statistical information. They talk of things such as money supply and average worker's wages. It is impossible to miss the fact that none of these discussions have anything to do the plight of the human who does not have enough money to eat. I finished my story by telling Peter that the most powerful economic action that these great leaders actually achieve at these lavish gatherings to discuss economic inequality is when they tip the waiter. I told him this might be the only action that fits what you and I might deem as experience. This story birthed a password between the two of us. When we would see someone agonizingly explaining something in the most statistical, theoretical, and non-experiential terms we would say, "Don't forget to tip the waiter!"

In order to understand that you are in a story, and indeed are the story, it is necessary to reorder your cognition to make it so. And what pointers keep you moving into a felt experience of story? One of these is simply to see that you and your story are tangible. That is to say, that they really happen. You may cognize them in a way that cuts you off from the potential that they hold. But you are extracting from a collection of arising pieces of manifestation. In this sense you are squarely placed in the story, experiential or emotional field. And part of your scanning system needs to include the awareness that this is actually where you are located. For when you wander into the wilderness of mathematical and statistical theory, all the while believing it to be reality, you need to know that you have wandered off the reservation. While your new story is deepening its experiential rooting, you want to keep it headed in that direction.

Remember when I talked about the cognition/story continuum akin to the time/space continuum of Einstein? Like our old golf grip, we begin to simply spin tales without utilizing the connective experience that is included in that continuum, even though we think we are saying something real. We are not. You likely would be surprised to know that the average adult holds a majority of stories that are merely notions as they have no tethering back to experience. This pointer is to push you back into including the experiential and emotional.

What I am saying here, in simple terms, is that we start our lives at the most authentic experiential and emotional place in our early years. We then learn to intellectualize and group elements that have zing and pop into boring statistical generalizations. We often call that education. We then come to a place where we know something is missing and we launch off on a journey as we call it. I am saying you have to start where you are and move back to the most vibrant pieces of life to approach awakening. So, we start in story at the dulled and intellectualized version we likely live within. Then we dig to the bottom where we begin to find our birthright of the original myth, our first story of cognition.

Think for a moment about the terms that we are considering. By linking the term 'field' to story, experience, and emotion, we are pointing to the tangible possibility of your own story. And we know that the natural movement of human maturity is towards the deepest and most authentic placement possible. Once there, you will find the bubbling up of emotion and experience. Those are elements of your story, which is how you would cognize those pieces of emotion and experience. Part of the journey that is *Story Theory* is to begin the noticing of these elements as you stand in the tangible field that is you. Many folks utilize a plethora of terms to describe this place. Consciousness, and even my term manifestation, are the current coin of the developmental kingdom. But do those story terms, if we could call them that, really call into your sense of reality something that is tangible and real? For most folks I have found that they do not. But when you begin to hold that your journey is tangible, and is here and is now, those faraway words begin to have a sense. And when your felt sense of standing in the story field is the same as standing in an alfalfa field, you are in the journey of *Story Theory*.

Let me take you back for a visit with my Grandpa. I love these stories as they are from my early life. This type of story is a great place for you to return as the elements of the field were in play when the story happened. Now this story looks to all the world like a teaching for a man coming of age, and it is that. But look closer and see that this wise man was calling out elements that pointed me to the bottom. I had learned as a young man how to become what others expected. Now, my Grandpa was taking me back to my roots. He knew there was a grounding in his grandson that had, through his conditioning and upbringing, been overlayed with intellectualization. Enjoy this one.

At the age of 18 months my family moved from Oakland to San Diego, California. My Grandfather was to become one of the founders of a new Pontiac dealership in Downtown. My mother was barely 19 at the time and she and I lived above the garage of our first Mission Hills home. Across the backyard, however, was the main house in this adobe style Spanish home that was so popular in the 50's in Southern California. This old place stood in Mission Hills looking out on the bay. It was the perfect combination of ocean and plant life. I loved them both. I will always remember how the smooth plastered walls magically gave off heat into the small hands of a young boy long after the sun had set. The trees would broadcast their dense smells into the air, as if asking me to investigate the blossoms and often fruit that hid among the branches. And if this were not enough, the long staircase of beautiful wood in the main house with carpeted steps seemed to reach into heaven. It smelled wonderfully old. At the top laid Grandma's trunk with special Grandma stuff inside. My Grandma, Grandpa, Aunt and Uncle all lived in the main house, which smelled like heaven when the kitchen was in full swing. It was a boy's dream, complete with dairy delivered bottles of chocolate milk, you know the kind with the metal cap, weekly. Outside of the kitchen was the crown jewel of our family, my Grandma's rose garden.

Before I launch into the story, you need to know about my Grandpa. He had three children, the oldest of which was my Mom. My Uncle Jerry, some 15 years older than me, was his only son. Grandpa was the quintessential Northern California intellectual, albeit with a modicum of grit. He rarely, if ever, got angry. He had graduated from the University of San Francisco in its first ever class. He went on to become a CPA with General Motors and worked in the car business his entire life. But things happen along the way, and into this perfect life was delivered his first grandson. That would be me! Grandma used to say that it was the only time in his career that he would be at home daily at 5 pm sharp. He hadn't got to spend the time he wanted with his own son and he was determined this would not happen again. And double duty he would do, as my Mom was single with me. Grandpa was the only game in town. Make no mistake, my Grandpa was my superhero and mentor. Our relationship was one of conspiracy in every regard. We had our stories, our adventures and even a nickname, Chuck, for the child who did not like his name. Why Chuck? It seems I liked that name and that was good enough for Grandpa.

At 5 pm every evening our adventure would begin. I can remember waiting for the last minutes before five, which stretched into eternity for a small boy. And then at last, there he was. It was on one of these nights that he and I were tasked with cleaning up the dog poop in the back yard. Grandpa loved dogs and that love was generously passed on to me. On this particular evening, Grandpa told me that poop was a wonderful fertilizer and that, even though Grandma wouldn't like it, we would sneak it into her beloved rose garden. We had to be very quiet, and we could get the job done. Of course, Grandma could look right out her kitchen window and inevitably we were caught. Grandma, the Danish freight train version, bolted out of the door to let us know, in no uncertain terms, that dog poop did not belong in her garden. Once she was back in the house my Grandpa conspiratorially whispered that we had been caught this one time, but it was only a practice round. Proudly, we knew another day would deliver us the victory our little crew so richly deserved.

So, what does this have to do with presence? My beloved Uncle Jerry passed late last year, and he knew that this story had always been a delight to me. And in one of our last conversations, he asked me if I would like to hear the whole story? I did not know there was a missing part, so I eagerly asked to hear. It turns out that my Grandma knew the whole time what my Grandpa had planned. Both of them loved the way in which Grandpa and I held our secrets between us, and Grandma had simply played the perfect role. Her speech to the two of us was all for show and in the service of supporting the conspiracy of the dog poop. Jerry told me that later that night when I was fast asleep, Grandpa went out and dug up the poop and made sure it was properly disposed. Why did they do such a thing?

Presence is simply the broadcast of authenticity as it blossoms from consciousness itself. If the adult uses a story to follow back to the roots and reclaim a lost authenticity, the child can simply retain it from the beginning. What does that take? It takes an environment of support and staging for that retaining to happen. It takes the wisdom of older generations to blatantly encourage the natural emergence in children rather than the rote conditioning that so often clips the wings of the little ones. I will never know if my grandparents knew this or simply held it as intuition. Whichever it was, they certainly knew that Grandpa and his sidekick Chuck would be supported at every turn and in every adventure. Dog poop and rose gardens, as silly as they seem as teaching devices, were just fine to assure that their grandson always had the channel open to what came in from the beyond.

Even if you do not have a history of support in your childhood that is fine. You have one now. Wisdom keepers and sages perform the same duty as a child's grandparents would. They walk along with you and point out things along the way. Papaji used to tell folks, "Be quiet and come to Satsang". This was his main pointer. This is all we are doing here together. Notice how I say things over and over again? Your loving supporters will always do that as they know it is hard to embrace what is new and unknown. Repetition is an act of love in this walk through the garden. Sure, your adult mind says, "Damn, this dude says the same thing over and over again". Fair enough. Has your adult mind grasped its portion yet? Has that translated into the apperception of awakening? If not here is my advice. Wash, rinse and repeat.

part four

Facing Life

chapter twenty

———•◦⧛◦•———

The grittiness of Life and zorba the Buddha

T HE GRITTINESS OF LIFE is simply a pointer. Why would this be important? For most folks, the constructed concepts of intellect have long ago been conflated with the juice of life itself. When they decide to take a spiritual journey, the tendency is to do it in the comfy confines of their own head, as it were. All pointers are in the service of creating a living understanding. The emphasis here is on living. And if one cannot tell the difference between living and dead, dead being what the intellect produces, then Zorba is a wonderful place to begin to learn. In Zorba's own words:

> *"I felt once more how simple a thing is happiness: a glass of wine, a roast chestnut, a wretched little brazier, the sound of the sea. Nothing else. And all that is required to feel that here and now is happiness in a simple, frugal heart."*
>
> ZORBA THE GREEK, 1964

At the age of 11, I saw the movie *Zorba the Greek* for my very first time. What appeared to most as black and white insanity planted its story seed deep within a young boy of the 60's. Anthony Quinn and Zorba himself were one and the same. This was life lived to its deepest possibility, based on nothing else than the possibility as it existed in the present moment. It did not feel spiritual, it did not look spiritual, but it was deeply profound.

Zorba, you see, was a Greek peasant and also a musician. His story takes place in a country village much like the one I was raised. He was gruff, loving and never passed an opportunity to take on life at its fullest. It was clear that the past and the future were never considerations for this fearless flyer in emotional airspace.

Many years later, I embarked on a journey to find the missing in myself. I had no idea what that was, but like Zorba I charged on. My journey took me to an ashram in India where a provocateur leprechaun named Osho was fast at work infuriating those who claimed to be his followers. One of his favorite metaphors was that of Zorba the Buddha. He sneered at the spiritual elite that believed themselves to have finished with the fray we all commonly called life. Osho was insistent that life, like a lemon, was intended to be squeezed to its last drop. And the squeezing was always, here, now, and never to be ignored. I immediately knew I had arrived at a place perfect for me. If squeezing life like a lemon was a starting place to a spiritual journey, I had a 35-year head start.

Grittiness is what we call this lemon squeezing. The

kind that Zorba would have understood and Osho rec-
ommended. It is also what is disappearing in our current
information age. This kind of pointer asks not about the
theory of economic inequality and the millions of Google
references that go with it. But what you, yourself, do when
faced with a hungry man on the street with no money.

In that Indian ashram I began the Buddha portion of
training, but I never forswore the roots of my original story as I held it then. I had climbed the corporate mountain; I had wrestled life and knew I would wrestle it again.
But now was time to look deep inside and understand the
missing part of the journey as I had taken it to this point.
And when I had emerged from the process called awakening, the nagging and incessant question would continually
arise, "Now what?" It was then that I recognized in the
rearview mirrors that my concepts would have the flavor
of the story that called me into action. And thus, began
the incessant digging to find the deepest and most original
story that I was. It was true that the secrets of awakening
were ever present. But I had been built to be a Zorba, a
warrior, and a man that gets things done. I did not belong
in a flock of fart dimples that blew smoke in each other's
direction as though Vedic philosophy and a relic in Turin
made a difference to a homeless man on the street. These
self-congratulating metaphysical posers talked as though
they knew my streets. But those were my streets. They still
are. And if a story makes no difference there, in my book it
is not a story. My mentors poured their souls into me. They
were different than me, but they knew what they were do-

ing. They did not shrink from unleashing the most powerful version of whom they saw in front of them. In fact, they often cajoled, pushed, insulted, and even laughed in order to surface any and every possibility. So, what is grittiness to me? It is finding the deepest story within anyone who dares to share my presence. It is unrelenting, uncompromised, and filled with the clarity that our world so deftly deflects and avoids at all costs.

GRITTINESS COINCIDES WITH THE BASEMENT OR ORIGINAL MYTH STORY

Yep. Books are filled with other's stories and intellectual constructions. You and I can use other people's stories but that is not real, living or useful in a search of this kind. In order to pass on the deepest level of felt experience, you must find, live and share your own basement story. Stop for a second and realize that you know what it is. Find and feel the depth in this story. Bring your own deep story into play. Nope, it is not in your head. You do not have to think, rather simply follow what wants to happen. Your story already knows itself with no script necessary.

So, what does this deep dive look like? It is the *Hero's Journey* as pointed to by one of my favorites, Joseph Campbell. But it is not the description I just burped out. Rather it is the descent into the basement of your own being. This is the place where your story of origin emerged. Where does it take you? To a felt experience of your original myth and story. And you may never have revisited the basement since you moved upstairs at some young age. What does this journey of descent look like? Here is my version and a story that may serve as a call to begin your own journey. It was June of 1991, a time of full monsoon in the country of India. As I emerged with my mind on fire from Buddha Hall in Poona, India, the muddy roads began their gleeful assault on this California desert kid. During the monsoon months it is not unusual that 20 or more inches of rain fall in one day in the various cities of India. But nothing could deter this hero on his way to, once again, reinvent the structure for the entire body of human knowledge, to create a "Theory of Everything". You think I am kidding? Not for a moment. I thought I was chosen to attain this never before imagined feat. How did it get this way for me? A couple of years earlier I had made the decision to leave my burgeoning corporate career in the quest of what I called "the search for truth". Of course, I attacked this new mountain in exactly the same way that I had climbed those in the past. First, I would assemble all of the known knowledge in the category of action that I had chosen to undertake. Then I would unleash those concepts on the unwieldy animal of experience and through the pure power of will, force it to submit. For sure this worked on school degrees, CPA exams and multi-million-dollar merger-acquisition deals. I was sure that enlightenment would fit the same category as hard-core achievement. And to do that it was obvious that assembling a unified body of human knowledge would surely do the trick.

To my delight, upon my arrival in India I found out

that, nightly in the ashram, an Osho discourse would run for a couple of hours. This amazing guru would discuss the various points of view and experiences of folks such as the Buddha, Lao Tzu, Zarathustra, Jesus Christ and Gandhi, to name a few. Many of my personal favorites were philosophers such as Heidegger, Nietzsche, and Kant. As I began to absorb these lectures, I would find myself running home at night and spending until the wee hours integrating what I had learned into my entire body of philosophy. I literally carried a model of what I considered to be the theory of everything in my head. For hours I would stare into the air, adding and deleting theoretical pieces as though they were car parts! I assumed that I had been called to construct such a thing. Of course, this became a day-by-day, unending, and eternal task. You see, I had chosen to take the concepts of the famous mystics, philosophers, and seers and mold them structurally, creating what I assumed to be reality itself. My suspicion was that consciousness was an amalgamation of the entire and properly ordered content of the universe. The whole must be made of all its parts.

There was one problem, however. No matter my valiant effort, the discrepancies in tone and definition could never come near to being overcome. When Buddha spoke, it was different than Heidegger. And when Gandhi spoke, I could always find something contrary in the words of Jesus Christ. And so, the stories of each of these great vessels of wisdom stood apart from each other. And finally, in frustration, I gave up on the idea that a single essence could underlie all of the stories that I had heard.

What could have gone wrong? Surely there is a way to get there.

In all of this I often thought back to the movie *Star Wars*. I knew that this was a quintessential tale lifted from Joseph Campbell's *Hero's Journey* and rendered into 1975 sci-fi. I remembered when Luke was being given lessons on how to deal with the force. Try as he might, he could not control it. And yet, gradually, in experience, something began to change. It was in that change that the mentor Obi-Wan had spun his Merlin's magic. I was the hero in my own seeker's journey and much like Luke, I was not getting it!

The good news in all of this is that I never gave up on the compelling need that had me spend those years in India. Life had thrust me into this search and it still beckoned me to find an answer to a question that seemingly had never been asked. And the seasoning of experience and the blessing of sitting at the feet of these masters, my mentors, had its impact. Soon after experiencing the pointers of my mentor and friend, Ramesh Balsekar, an awakening occurred that melted the so-called particulars of consciousness, concepts included, into the essence of which I am. In fact, what we all are.

It was not long until I could look into my own seeker's journey and begin to understand the daunting barriers that face those who search. And as I did so, I began to notice that what had been the separate and varied voices of the masters and mentors in the past now were simply a symphony that carried a single tune. No longer did I start at a particular concept as spoken or written and pull it from without into a single theory. No, now I was a conduit from the basement through which the power of authentic story emerged in its unique version of truth, delivered in its own authentic way. I had my way and they had theirs, but these ways all emerged from the same original ground. There never really was a difference, if viewed from the bottom. It is much like every snowflake has its own particular and unique design. And yet, each one is exactly the same in its 'snowness'. In fact, it was evident that understanding always arises from reality and never the other way around. Holy shit, I had been forcing when I should have been responding! Much like Luke, the world stood on its head. I was but a part of what wanted to happen. And I was not in charge of the ride, I was just being asked to play my part. It was not, "May the force be with you" it was, "May you be with the force".

This was where all the mentors had always been pointing. And, as in the famous Buddha story, I was too busy looking at their fingers rather than to where they pointed! For those who do not remember, Buddha was famous for telling his followers that when he pointed to something that they needed to look where he indicated, not at the finger that he used to point with.

In the hero's journey there comes a point where the warrior/hero steps into a very special place. His mentor cannot accompany him there. It looks to the entire world that the protagonist has isolated himself from every possibility of help. And in this moment, he is drawn to who he really is. And he finds that everyone, his mentor included, has always been exactly who he is. He has never been alone. That moment delivers to him the illusory nature of separation, rendering it ineffective, as all illusions are. And from that moment on he no longer draws from the outside in, but rather gathers from the roots as if from the basement below. And delivers his story as the conduit he is, a powerful message of himself he cannot resist. And what does he learn?

He learns that the basement story of his being is beneath and beyond all other stories he knows. It repels comparison and is the root of all the fragments he once thought was powerful in itself. He also knows that gathering the content of others can quite simply choke out the rooted original creation that wants to blossom forth. And so, he must demand that he, himself, stand in the authenticity of pure creation as simply a vessel of what is being called. This knowing is a felt experience and once felt, never forgotten. It is grittiness itself before it has been grated into the pablum we call intellectual construction. Life is real and consciousness is gritty, not an edited podcast. Find that realness and then let the story channel itself. This is the pointer to a living understanding.

THE HERO DISAPPEARS

Many spiritual teachers, myself included, use the *Hero's Journey* as a pointer. The activity of moving from the knowledge platform to the wisdom path holds much of what it looks like to seek spiritually. The caring that pours out from a teacher who wants to give the seeker anything that will make the journey understandable. But there is one more point that can be easily missed in all of this. *The Hero's Journey*, as we all have inherited it from folks like Jung and Campbell, lives entirely in the concept of ego. The modern philosophies and psychologies never imagined something beyond ego. Only in the entrance to spiritual seeking or mysticism does the notion that ego is a lived concept arise.

You now know that both Stephen Covey and Peter Drucker were mentors of mine in the period before I left for India to see Osho. Both men were beyond excited that I had chosen, as it looked to them, to pursue something clearly outside of what normally would be considered a business career. At first, I was not sure what to make of this overt outpouring of support. But then one day Stephen took me by the shoulders and looked deeply in my eyes. "Alan", he said, "mentors, good ones that is, always expect their acolytes to surpass them. Not in prowess or attributes but in pushing into the unknown in a way that will continue to explode the revelation of who we are. You are now taking off from the nest and I expect you to come back and tell me what my work will now become in your hands."

When I returned from my years in India I did, indeed, have the chance to continue my conversations with Stephen. He marveled that within the spiritual process that "beyond ego or self-mastery" was even possible. His work had always centered on the polishing of the ego for both leadership and self-improvement outcomes. He would have never imagined something beyond that. That beyond was a place where the actual perception of the arising world was yielding totally different outcomes, outcomes he never thought imaginable. He immediately saw that the *Hero's Journey* must include a further chapter. Yes. Every corporate tool for individual composition was based on Jung's archetypal stories and by extension the *Hero's Journey*. But never had there been an instance that the Hero himself simply disappeared as an operable autonomous author of his own story. Now the simple idea that consciousness itself lived each body-mind and all of our intellectual equipment was navigational and not decisional was both groundbreaking and breathtaking. In our last conversation, Stephen shared with me that our relationship had yielded the golden outcome of mentorship. The teacher's shoulders had been stood upon to deliver the thing that the mentor would have never imagined. You see, in a certain way, we were in the *Hero's Journey* and the mentor had disappeared.

I must add that there is a connection here to presence. Before I left, Stephen and I often discussed what presence was. We had a pointer phrase that we shared which is "Belonging in the Room". We both noticed in corporate leadership that presence could always be experienced and seemingly always by a leader who "belonged in the room". Now, Stephen and I had been in many a meeting together as we had served on a board together at the School of management at BYU. This was well in advance of my Hero's Journey to India. Belonging in the room was presence and we never let each other forget that knowing. However, there came a time when I returned from India and had experienced the awakening moment. One day, I went to see Stephen in his office at BYU and as I entered the room he looked deeply in my eyes. He said, "Alan, I love this notion of the Hero disappearing in his final spiritual quest. You and I have often seen these heroes before that venture and said they belonged in the room. I now see something a little bit different and I am updating our pointer. You, indeed, have disappeared and it is there for all to see. I no longer see you as belonging in the room for now you have become the room itself."

Grittiness, simplicity, and being. These are the attributes that spin out of presence itself. All there is, is consciousness. And you are that consciousness.

chapter twenty-one

——•◦ ⚬◌⚬ ◦•——

Death is the poster boy for separation

PERHAPS THE BIGGEST elephant in the room for humanity is that of death. Irvin D. Yalom, in his classic *Existential Psychotherapy*, posits that the field of psychology simply misses and does not account for the deep existential issues of humanity itself. Like my story about Mulla Nasruddin, who is looking for a lost key but in the wrong place, says, "We are looking here, not where I lost the key, but where there is good light!" And what is the number one existential issue? You guessed it, death. There is no single event in the course of a human life that is more central to behavior than death. In fact, many seekers are such for the simple reason that they intuit that death of a physical body cannot possibly mean the end to who they sense they are. Society and culture create religions, rituals, philosophies, and structure all legal and political policies around death. But do they even know what dies? Are they even looking in the right place? I am not sure it matters. The freak out from simple stories of death are enough to send humanity in general running. Like Pascal's wager, let's organize around anything that could be true no matter the odds!

What does awakening and the spiritual quest have to do with all of this? Everything. Let's review and walk ourselves right into the illusion and fallacy of death. In *Story Theory* we learn two things. First is the nature of story, how it is created and where it lives. Secondly, we come to understand that we reclaim or follow our own story back to the original myth version. Then there is one more step to take. The very last step is to see that you are not your story. Let's dive into the notion of death.

The reason for seeking is a result of our own misidentification of who we really are. This misidentification is a result of a belief that we are separate entities roughly defined by our body-minds. To do this, we have to extract what we believe ourselves to be from all else in manifestation. Then we assign attributes to ourselves as separate entities and attributes to all the other separate things as well. We create a story, or we could say a character in a script of other characters and objects. We then conflate that story and assume it is who we are. What goes wrong here? This conflation opens the door to the possibility that "who we are" has a beginning and an end. If it is possible that you end, isn't it reasonable to be afraid of that end? It certainly is. But notice that the whole proposition of awakening in consciousness includes the obvious. The awareness that we are, ultimately is eternal. It is that which is aware, has always been aware, and will always be aware. This awareness is an unbroken whole. It is the screen upon which all arises and appears.

When the arisings have ended, the screen will still be.

It is easy to see the misidentification and supposition that we are roughly the body-mind, as opposed to all that exists, is dependent on extracting ourselves from our background. Extraction is a separating activity, and in that separation, we deduce that we can begin and we can end just like any body-mind obviously does. In one fell swoop we have added separation and its ever-present sidekick, fear. It takes a separate entity with an impending end to generate the fear that that end will indeed occur.

What is the principal teaching of our entire life handed to us by society, culture and family? We are incessantly taught that we are an autonomous separate author of our own actions. How does every individual act? They act "as if" that were true. Life is a choreography of separation imprinted on us in every moment. Even language itself gets into the act by not only facilitating transactions between body-minds but imprinting that separating facilitation as if it were true.

Many folks can become confused by this notion. Does this mean that the body-mind does not feel and participate in the pain and sadness of death? After all, awakening is the proper identification of who we really are and is a perfect peace in everyday living. Doesn't that awakening eliminate the impact of death? The answer to this query is the inevitable, "yes and no". Yes, it is seen in self-realization that you are the awareness within which the body-mind, or your story identity, appears. That apperception bestows the sense of permanent peace. But it does not eliminate the experience that happens to each character within the drama script of life. Each actor plays his or her role, including all of the feelings that are included in their part. So. Yes, the pain and sadness of death come with death. But the fear that we will somehow end or cease to exist is seen through.

A couple of years back I moved to the big island of Hawaii. For the two years before that I was shuttling back and forth to the island to build the house in which I now live. I would go over for 2-3 weeks at a time every month or so. I would meet with the various contractors and provide any help needed as this went on for that two years. One evening after I had arrived at my lodging and after dinner, I received a phone call. It went like this. "Mr. Shelton, Your son has suffered a terrible fall from a serious height. He is in the emergency room in a coma, and we aren't sure he will make it until morning. We want to make sure you know this has occurred." As most fathers who have received such a call, this is an intense moment. It turns out that my son, Michael, had slipped on the stairway of his 3rd story apartment. As he grabbed for the railing it gave way as it had been installed in the 30's when the building was constructed. From this height, Michael was about 40 feet above the concrete driveway below. Luckily, there was an overhang over the entrance to the garage about 12 feet before the ground which he hit on the way down. It broke his fall and ultimately saved his life. Michael suffered 4 skull fractures, 6 breaks in his pelvis and an assortment of other broken bones. At the emergency room they drilled one side of his skull to relieve the internal pressure from his swelling brain, hoping they would not have to drill the other side. They then induced a medical coma hoping this would give him a chance at survival. It was at this point that I was informed of his condition. Even knowing I was but an actor in the drama did not reduce the intensity of what a father feels in these kinds of moments.

I remember vividly that after the call I sat down on my bed and simply closed my eyes to be with the news. I knew that by the next dawn that it was possible I would lose my son. The emotion was overwhelming. I did, however, know something more. My son was exactly who I am in consciousness. His body-mind began, and it would end. For both of us and for you as well, it is simply a matter of how and when. In other words, the story identity called Michael was as any other story identity. In the middle of that mind numbing experience, I knew that there was no way I was losing anything. My story was and always had been a series of beginnings and endings. And who I really was had neither of those. Within the permanent peace of that knowing arose the maelstrom of a possibly dying son.

Often the stories of my mentors feel as though they are my own. Ramesh Balsekar relates an occasion when a stricken father visited Nisargadatta Maharaj, his guru, around 1980. This man had lost his own son in a car accident just some days earlier. He indicated that he had attempted all of the usual ploys to console himself, but he found it impossible to meet this event with philosophic fortitude. He told Nisargadatta that he kept coming back to the tragedy of cruel fate that deprived him of his son in the prime of his son's life. He simply could not get over his grief. It was here that Nisargadatta revealed the missing component of this father's understanding and walked him through to a new possibility. Does such a walkthrough eliminate the sorrow, unmitigated as it is initially, from the experience of a father. No, it does not. But it does allow the sorrow to have its sway and then transform. Here is how Nisargadatta approached this man.

He told the man that he assumed he was not there for sympathy as he must have received all he needed thus far in that category. What he proposed was a new perspective. He then asked if this father had the courage to live his life with this new understanding or was he intent on wallowing in his grief, as he called it. Upon hearing this the man immediately asked what he should do. The answer was that there was nothing to do other than consider this new perspective. He needed to see the transient as the transient and the real as real.

And what was that? Nisargadatta went on to explain that the transient view is that he and his wife had created a child, but that creation was a chance or transient event. Had they made an agreement with someone that they would have a son? A particular body? A particular destiny? Wasn't the conception itself a chance event? That the fetus survived the hazards of the womb also the same? Essentially this man's son was a chance event, one over which he had no control, and this event had come to an end. This is the view from the transient, false and unreal.

So, what is the real viewpoint? The viewpoint that always has been the case and always will be the case? Realize that you are not a person. There literally is no individual other than in your imagination or story world as I would call it. The self ends up being a victim to this illusion of individuality. Consciousness, itself, mistakenly believes that there is such a thing and separates you from the world you live within. Change your viewpoint. Do not see the world as something outside of yourself, see the person you imagine yourself to be as part of all that arises. You are pure awareness and from that apperceptive viewpoint you are beyond time, space and ultimately invulnerable to any experience. Yes, you will see the experience of overwhelming grief fill the screen upon the moment of the death of a loved one. But that arising will also fall as it ultimately does not belong to you. You see, there is no "you" as you believe and act as if were the case.

The man went away happy to have been afforded another viewpoint in his process of grief.

Death is the centerpiece of our culture and the bedrock of separation and fear. When we misidentify with our story self it is easy to see that the story will come to an end. Then the entirety of mankind holds hands, in the illusory individuated version, and tells one another, "We are all gonna die". Even when our intuition senses that there is something wrong with this conclusion the cacophony of humans in fear drown out the quiet intuitive voice.

The spiritual journey is the possibility of dissolving this illusion. I will never forget hearing Amrito speak to the throngs on the day of Osho's death. Amrito was Osho's personal doctor and as he began to cry minutes before Osho's passing, Osho immediately grabbed the moment and said to Amrito, "No, no, that's not the way". He then went on to say, "I leave you my dream". The apperception of manifestation through Osho saw that there was nothing dying, and anything left behind was but a dream. That is the entire possibility of awakening. Death is the poster boy for separation and fear, wound up in an illusion that has been carried by humanity since the beginning. Awakening has always been there before death and will be after death.

chapter twenty-two

Duality, Relaxation and the Ego

PERHAPS THIS IS THE time notice how life is happening around us. Many see these detail and perhaps philosophical dissections to be boring and tedious. I suppose that might be so. But bear with me as I want to point out a few understandings that will help you along the way. You might often hear the term duality. What is that and why is it important? Duality is simply the experience of perceiving difference. We could say that the minute a human looked outside of themselves and saw something that they cognized or extracted as different from themselves, duality was born. If the perceived world can go from unperceivable perfect unity without distinction to one of distinction, there now are two perceivable things. Then from two to three and three to four and into the billions! The world is immediately composed of differences. This is commonly called duality. You hear me drone on and on about separation. Can you see that separation is the foundation of perceiving distinct things? Good. From here let's orient ourselves around that notion to see what corollaries pop up. You might also hear the term dualism. Humanity is largely in agreement that they believe in dualism. Duality is the world appearing in components. Dualism is the belief that the only perceivable possibility is dualistic. That dogged belief is the one that immediately cuts us off from the examination of where the emergence of difference arises. Can there be a prior unity that is foundational to what we perceive? Of course, my response is, "Yes!" It is the abandonment of our holistic consciousness as a lived experience that thrusts the supposed separate ego into felt bondage. That sense of being cut off is the driver for seekers looking for awakening or enlightenment. Unfortunately, most look into the world of separation believing some distinct or separate truth or understanding will awaken them, but in their state of perceptive difference. They miss the piece that what they are, as an eternal essence, outside of the dualism. They have unconsciously come to believe that a world of differences is all there is. OK, we have made it to here!

What are some things we should know about our dual world and its inhabitants? In order to cobble different bits together there is a certain glue that is needed. What do I mean? Consider, for a moment, that our stories, concepts and the like are all constructions. We already covered a bit of that. We take pieces and cobble them together in our intellectual holdings from our perception of our world and voila, we have constructions. What holds constructions together? Glue, cement, nails, screws, etc. What do such things add to our equation? Tension. All parts in a construction have a tendency to move into their natural, distinct pieces. When we introduce a glue to that we are essentially forcing these pieces to combine into an amalgamation. That amalgamation is in tension and forcibly contained. All of your concepts, including the big one, your ego itself, live in this tension of assembly. That means that when I harp on about separation I am also harping on about this tension. Can you see that the belief of dualism sentences us all to a self-perception of tension? We see ourselves as the constructed ego story, not the foundational original self of pure consciousness. Our entire awakening journey is the reclaiming of that original state. The pointers I include are with the intent to stay aware of the possibility of our original self.

Now, remember that the ego is one of the concepts or stories that roam around in our world of difference. Stories are just animated concepts. There is a short instruction given centuries ago by one of the great enlightened masters. He would say that the ego was like a tiger in the corner of the room. He would further admonish, always keep your eye on that tiger for the minute you lose awareness of it you will be consumed by the tiger. In essence, humanity, in all of its wisdom, has elected to believe that the tiger simply is not there. We live in a world where the tiger has consumed all and now we feel in bondage and are asking why. Folks like me are pointing to the corner of the room and screaming, "There is the tiger!" The world of the tiger is tension. We want to leave that world and stay aware that we unconsciously will return if we do not pay attention.

All pointers to consciousness, which do not and cannot live in the world of conceptual tension, are based in pure relaxation. It is your original state. Now can you see why we use pointers? We cannot use concepts to replace concepts and get relaxation. Concepts hold the glue called tension. There is no awakening in tension. There simply cannot be. So, we point out of the only and entire world we have constructed to a non-intellectual essence or experience that is relaxation.

Oftentimes, I am asked by followers for an exercise or practice to include in one's daily life to attempt to stay in awareness. Now this is a tricky ask. Let me tell you why. Practices and exercises are typically things done by whom? By your ego self. So, in prescribing such a thing we are heading down the path to creating a possibility that you will be continuously conditioned as an ego with a discipline, all the while pretending that the ego practice is one leading out of ego. Can you see that? Pointers intend on dissolving the glue that binds your concepts together in the hope that you will fall through to the foundation of pure consciousness that lies below. Make them a discipline and we blow up the very purpose. Again, why is that? By making pointers a discipline we introduce the glue of ego as the one doing the practice. What we want is to see through the ego by means of relaxation. Asking the ego to practice is akin to having the fox guard the henhouse.

As you know, I have been surrounded in my life by the great sages that had to confront this dicey proposition. What did these forebears suggest?

Sri Ramana Maharshi is one of the most revered and famous mystics that approached this issue. One of the little-known facts about his life is that he really only wrote a very few pages in his entire life. In 1902 he received some 20 plus questions and wrote 8 pages in response. That essentially is the entirety of his writing. What exercises or practices did he give his followers? Ramana would have his people do self-inquiry. This was simply asking oneself, "Who Am I?" Now, he meant for the acolyte to actually ask the question and then look inside for the answer. This was a tangible happening, not an intellectual process. Typically, a follower would generate large quantities of internal answers until a moment would come where they could see that there was no answer other than mind talk. The breakthrough here is that ultimately one could see that there is no "me" that lives outside of the mind. And that "me" can only be held in tension. Ramana, in his suggestion to do such inquiry, would warn all of his folks not to make this a practice or discipline. Why? I think you now know the answer to that one.

Another sage in the lineage of conceptual dissolution is Nisargadatta Maharaj. He is well known for the book *I Am That*. This spiritual classic is a composition of his speaking compiled by one of his followers. It is a translation as well, as Nisargadatta spoke no English and all of his outpourings are translated. His main advice dispensed in his Satsangs were to locate the essence of one's sense of existence. This is commonly called the first arising of "I Am". He would often say that his master told him to do one thing which was to find this sense of essence. Then the only thing was to constantly and simply sit on that essence. He would often tell folks that this was not an exercise or practice but rather a discovery which one could embrace once found. He was very aware that a practice could be an invitation for the tiger to consume.

As you know, I spent many an hour with Ramesh Balsekar. He was my beloved mentor in my movement on the spiritual journey. Ramesh, like me, lived largely in our modern world. He was the President of the Bank of India and a graduate of the London School of Economics. Like me, he was steeped in the rise of markets, finance, and digital platforms until his death in 2009. His approach leaned into the dissolution of our assumptive state of autonomous ego. His major exercise-like advisory to his people was to take 25 minutes at the end of any given day. They would begin the 25-minute period by locating the thing that happened that day they deemed to be the most obvious happening for which they themselves alone were responsible. Then he would ask them to identify all of the things that had to have also happened in order for the moment they had picked to have occurred. If they hadn't accidentally made a wrong turn, if they had eaten at their normal restaurant rather than the one they did eat at, etc., etc. He wanted them to see that the entire set of happenings over which they had no control were necessary for the happening of that which they claimed was their doing. How could they then claim in the end that anything was their doing? All of this was intended to induce the relaxation that we have already introduced here. Like the others, Ramesh would often advise that one should avoid having a practice or discipline and that this exercise should not be turned into one.

As you encounter the pointers contained in the reading here, realize that they are intended to dissolve your preconceived notion of yourself. Once dissolved, there is no reason to continue to engage with them. Do not make them a practice or discipline. But, what about meditation, you might ask. Meditation is intended to give you a taste of having the world of manifestation arise within you. It is attempting to place you outside of the ego even with the ego continuing to arise within. If one makes meditation a practice, what has happened now? The noticing of what is not within the ego has been placed within the ego. Not too bright, huh? I am often asked if I continue to meditate as a custom. My answer is why would one meditate when their life is now exactly what meditation seeks to induce? If your life is meditation, why would a practice that supports egoic movement be a part of that? You see? Practice and discipline are egoic executions and are tension held. We seek to dissolve that tension through pointers which point out of the world of tension into a perception of relaxation.

Many times, people notice that I live what appears to be a fairly normal and unremarkable life. I laugh, I cry, I love street food, and I am as Californian as they come. Typically, they will next comment, in what seems like confusion, "So a normal life continues as always within awakening?" The answer to that is, that it indeed does. I often say that the entire purpose of consciousness is to reveal itself to itself. All awakening does is create the permanent peace that is your birthright that you have walled off until now. That walling off is the intuitive source of your knowing that this work needs to be done. But once that birthright of collapsing into consciousness itself has happened, the world will continue much as it always has. But now there will be two apparent components that really are one. First is the human embrace of whatever is the revealing of consciousness itself. Second is the knowing that this embrace is simply held in a bigger version of who you are that you had not supposed was there, but actually will feel like coming home. For it is what you always have been.

As you go along on your seeking path you will likely notice that different things begin to happen. Things that did not happen before. It is not all that unusual for your normal perception to shift to an apperceptive mode. It will feel like you are now *within* the field you normally think is viewed by yourself. The sense will be that you are far away from the scene of action and that it is happening on its own. It turns out that it is! And there you are right in the middle of it as if you were in a movie being watched from afar. To be fair, the first time this happens you will never forget it. In fact, you likely will bring it back into your ego map and attempt to reproduce it. That is what I did for sure. This happening is called a free sample. That is the term Ramesh used and it is the best I have heard. This is simply one of the events that happen. But here is the trick. It is simply a happening and came to you without any trigger or action on your part. That is the way it came and that is the way it will always come, permanent or temporary. By now, you can take the essence of this writing and see that the last thing you would want to do is pull that happening back into your ego map and then attempt to reproduce it. Simply stay in the "I Am" or your sense of existence. Osho used to famously say, "Keep going". Do not forget the sense of it but also know that there is nothing you can do to make it happen. Here, again, notice that relaxation is the way forward which means stay open and available and simply wait and witness. Ramesh would often say that the mode of operation in the seeking experience was the feminine. Available, open, and watching are all descriptors of this non-activity. There is no efforting here.

Here is another little pointer that Ramesh used to toss in from time to time. He would speak of the "working mind" and the "thinking mind". As in all pointers, these are just stories intended to have you fall into the experience itself. So, here you have one story based on our normal modality of action, tension and separation - the thinking mind. On the other hand, you have the story of relaxation, letting it happen, and being lived which is the working mind. One story of the ego state and one story of the apperceptive state. My guess is that you have a pretty good idea of how the thinking mind works. You are tasked with deciding who in your company will get the next promotion. So, you immediately assess the history of that person within the company. Does she get along with folks in the organization, would it be politically advantageous to promote her or another person, how will it affect you, etc., etc.? Notice how the thinking mind revolves around the egos in play and how you have to analyze and position within your intellectual analysis. You likely do this in many, if not all, of your decisions. Then we have the working mind. Here the thinking happens for you. The notion of the advancement arises. The job is thus and such and the obvious candidate that is perfect for the job makes herself obvious. She just pops into view. In fact, many times you might have this obvious choice drop right into view but then you begin to grind and process comparing and assembling pieces and parts. Notice this if it happens, for you have just moved from the working mind to the thinking mind. The first thought was simply an appearing within perfect relaxation. The second required your autonomous ego to work hard and there was lots of heavy lifting. See the two stories here?

Pointers are intended not only to help understand the notion of your identified life and the reframing that happens once the split mind is dropped, but they also speak to your experience as you paddle through. Notice that this is all that is going on here. How do you get out of the hole? First, understand how and also what it will feel like as it happens. Get it? Awesome. Keep going!

chapter Twenty-Three

———•◦ ;◦; ◦•———

The Basic understanding

S OME TIME BACK I watched a piece on the new
gurus popping up all over the place in the New Age
world that has been around since the 60's. Well, guess
what? It has become quite a multi-billion-dollar thing. As I
watched, I could not help but notice how complicated the
spiritual awakening scene has become or possibly has been
all along. There are third eyes, harmonic energies, alien
channeling, oils and shamans galore and they all look like
updated hippies, for the most part, to me. It reminded me
of a story between Ramesh and a seeker. It goes like this…
After the end of one of the talks in California, one of the
visitors said to Ramesh, "This is my last day, at least in this
session. I am leaving this afternoon. When I go home, I
shall be asked about you and what you talked about. They
will think I am crazy if I tell them that you do not put on
any robes, that you speak perfect English, that you were
a bank president before you retired, and that your entire
teaching is based on one Truth that the entire manifestation
and its functioning is an entirely impersonal and self-gen-

289

erated process, and that the sentient beings are merely the instruments (without any volition) through which this process takes place."

Ramesh laughed and told him that what he said reminded him of a story he had come across some time ago: As a patient was about to leave a doctor's consultation room, the new patient spun around and shot the doctor a quizzical glance. The doctor asked her what the matter was, and she replied: "I don't know. I arrived five minutes early for my appointment. You took me in right away. You spent a lot of time with me. I understood every word of your instructions, and what is more, I can even read this prescription you wrote. Are you a real doctor?"

Much like Ramesh, here I sit with a pretty simple message. It is so simple that the circular nature of seeking seems like a playlist on repeat in much of my writing. It is all about mistaken identity as the seeker repeats the above in his own words. So here is more of that repetition in possibly a new approach reader wise.

Thus far in our journey together, I have concentrated on particular aspects of the spiritual process. Why have I written this way? In every unique period of history certain pointers are going to be more applicable. Currently, we live in a fast paced, information driven era of postmodern and identity thinking, for the most part. How the dissolution of held concepts on the part of the seeker can occur are dependent on how those concepts are constructed. We could say that this unique construction is a context. But wait, you might say. I thought there was a universal sense to all of this. Aren't seekers from time immemorial engaged in pre-cisely the same trek? Yes, yes, they are. But each of those have language, custom, society, and culture that lay down the boundaried structures within the stories that we live. Intellect itself is a certain kind of boundary, as we already know. The structures of intellect, those currently in play in our ethos, make that even more so.

In my travels, I have found that many of my readers want a wide-view lens of the field of spiritual movement. It seems to help to have that in order to drop in the piec-es I present that contextualize my writing. Until now I have never actually undertaken an exposition of the en-tire core teaching or basic understanding that is universal and non-contextual. What is that version which the Upani-shads, Buddha, Ramana, Nisargadatta, Osho and Ramesh would all claim lived in their teaching as well as the version I have presented? Well, here it is.

The central plank, and only one to worry about, is the knowledge of one's true identity. Everything else rotates around this axis. There is nothing more important or sa-lient in the spiritual exercise than this knowing. And here is the kicker. The only way to this tangible understanding is through intense and absorbed personal experience. You need both clarity and earnestness, or tenacity as we might call it, for self-knowledge. This requires a maturity of heart and mind which requires an application to daily life of whatever you have understood, no matter the amount. Whatever you do, do it wholesale. There is nothing that will derail your movement so much as compromise. Ultimately, these things I speak of are not a function of what "you" do but rather will be seen as simply arising in what you harvest as your story. Nonetheless, go for it resolutely until you see that it never was you. When it is seen as simply the way your story shows up you will understand the tangibility that looks to all the world as though it belongs to you, but it does not. I steal a term from Nisargadatta to describe this tangibility once seen which is apperception.

There is nothing in the study of religious texts or words of the masters that matter, for these are but "hearsay" as an attorney might call them. Even intellect cedes its so-called necessity in this awareness. The only incontrovertible foundational bedrock on which one can stand is within tangible experience. This immediately eliminates assumptions, concepts, stories and speculations as none of this will collapse into your birthright of identity. In fact, as you know, we seek to collapse all of those things in the hope that a tangible phenomenal event can occur.

So, how do we have that conversation, eliminating the fluff and relying only on personal experience? Firstly, you know that you are here. Then you know I am here. We could add that there is a world outside. Finally, we could also conclude that there was some creator of all of this. These are the only critical elements to the awakening conversation. You, yourself, can now eliminate the hearsay of all the crap you have found in spiritual texts, on your so-called spiritual journey thus far, and well-meaning guides who have knowingly or unknowingly given nothing but hearsay. Our conversation needs no words or experience from someone else. There is no certificate to obtain that will certify your evolved state. It is just you, here and now. Strip and disabuse yourself of the sense that you are an educated person and the need to impress others that comes with that sense. You are now starting from scratch. Every time you hear a pointer go back to that scratch. That is the only place that really matters, and it is the starting place every time. In fact, your journey will deposit you right there in the very end anyway.

Now that we have that established, let's ask a few simple questions. What is it that without which no one would be able to perceive anything or do anything? That which is necessary to be able to ask questions of me or anyone else? And without which I would not be able to answer such questions? Let's call that "without which" consciousness. If you and I were not conscious could we even have this conversation? So, let's dig a bit further. What is this thing we have labelled consciousness? Could it be anything other than the sense of being alive, the sense of being present? It is the sense of conscious presence. This sense does not really have a reference to any individual being present. It is simply conscious presence as such. Then peruse a bit more. Without this consciousness, such as when this presence leaves the body at death, the body is quickly jettisoned. It usually is buried or cremated. The body without consciousness is simply a stench center. One is left to ask, "Where is the individual who was there when consciousness was present?" Most will say that he has died. He could have been a leader in his time. But now he is gone? What is really gone?

Throughout the ages of mystical inquiry, the notion of "I Am" has been tagged as this sense of presence, or the juice of life, called consciousness. Recognizing that this consciousness must be there before anything else can be, we can be certain that this is the entire subject matter of our search. One must be conscious before the world even appears and is perceived by them. Resultantly, inquiries about anything else are essentially useless until the dive into consciousness has occurred.

What then are the basic questions we consider in this encounter with consciousness? From whence does it come? Does it have a source? If so, what is it? What supports it? And what is its nature? These lead to true wisdom. Without consciousness there can be nothing phenomenal, no existence. This has to be the highest order of what anyone can conceive and must be the highest God that is possible. Remember, this is based on just the few particulars we cite above. Sure, humans give essences, seen or unseen, names. Ignoring such naming and other intellectual add-ons, this presence must be of the highest order. When presence leaves the body there is no individual, no world and no God.

This relationship between the body and consciousness must be clearly perceived. Without consciousness the body is simply dead material. Nisargadatta would say that the body was the food that sustains consciousness and the instrument through which consciousness functions. He would go on to say that consciousness is the nature, suchness, or taste of the physical body much like sweetness is to sugar.

Now think a minute about how your body with consciousness came about. What is its source? That is easy. The source of the body is the male sperm fertilized in the ovum of the womb of a female body. Consciousness must be latent within. It is this very fertilized ovum latent with consciousness that grows in the mother's womb. It is delivered in due course as a baby, grows into childhood, and through the span of life. What is the impetus behind this growth? Nothing other than consciousness latent in the womb, which itself is nothing more than the essence of food consumed by the parents. It must be that consciousness is the very nature of the body, the sweetness of sugar, as Nisargadatta would have said. Further, the body is made of and sustained by food. Where in all of this do we find the individual? Nowhere. In fact, the individual has no significance in all of this whatsoever. The body is made of food and consciousness is universal and all pervading. How could the individual be anything but illusory and how could it claim a separate existence, bondage or liberation for itself? Much like an author of a play, humans have written appendages to just what we know for ourselves. And the result, which they refer to as "you", is of the same order as those written roles. They are stories.

How could this individual have been consulted regarding his birth? His birth to a certain set of parents? But wait. We already know that the "me" and "mine" have come about after the birth. Birth, itself, is all the result of a natural process over which neither the child nor parents have any choice. All that is here is a body created from food and a universal consciousness which lives post latency in the body until it is released at death into universal and impersonal consciousness. Where in all of this are "you"? You were not a party to the creation of the phenomenal unit you have been told that "you" are. All you know is that your parents told you that "you" were born, and this body is "you". You have no experience of "your" birth.

The question, as always, becomes, "Who are you?" You are what you were before the body came into being and what you will be after its disposal. You are what you were a hundred years ago and what you will be a hundred years from now.

Now comes the fun part. Who, then, is acting in the world as a body? Yep, you guessed it! In manifestation consciousness is everything. It is this consciousness that acts through billions of bodies. It does so in accordance with the body and mind of the body. It simply manifests through the hardware and software of each organism. We know that there are no two bodies, or even snowflakes for that matter, that are alike. In other words, the temperament and character of each body-mind, based on its physical composition and conditioning, form a hardware/software combination that functions as consciousness propels it through its rounds.

If this is clearly understood, then that clarity should make it obvious that there is no individual that could have the autonomy to act on its own. However, the individual, in his ignorance, believes that it is "he" who acts. He takes delivery of actions that take place, binds himself in illusory bondage, and suffers pain and pleasure. This is how bondage comes to be.

Ramesh Balsekar would often call the intellect a "dubious gift". Why? Because it takes the intellect to create the notional bondage we seem to believe has befallen us. It advises us that we are somehow a special being apart from all of the remainder of creation. But as far as the physical features of the construct are concerned, there is no difference between any of the various kinds of sentient creatures. The process might differ slightly, but the tangibility is the same.

Perhaps looking at this will help to understand the role of impersonal consciousness in all of this. What is our true identity? Unmanifested, in stillness and silence, our identity is the absolute. Other terms often used include prior unity, pure awareness not aware of itself, consciousness at rest, and source. However, this unmanifested does leap into a manifestation. Why? There is no "why". Causality is a feature of duality. This duality is an extension of pure awareness, as time and space are manifested from the ineffable and unmanifested purity. Once this happens then impersonal consciousness projects itself into seeking itself as the "other". This is just a temporary extrusion. It could be said that personal living is akin to a temporary illness, without cause or reason, as part of the total functioning of the impersonal consciousness in its role as consciousness in action. The imagery in the Upanishads might be helpful here. Many experts date them to 1000 BC but it is well known that the oral tradition that carried them might well have been in play up to twenty thousand years prior. Whatever the dates, absolute impersonal consciousness is seen as a spider. Roughly, "Just as a spider spins forth its thread and draws it back again, the entirety of creation is woven from the absolute and unto it returns."

It is in this way that each phenomenal form, that is you and me, lives out the allotted duration and at the end of the life arc disappears as spontaneously as it appeared. Consciousness as an object is relieved of its physical limitations and, no longer conscious of itself, merges into awareness. Essentially, one neither is born nor do they die. And consciousness, entirely unperturbed, continues creating new forms and destroying old ones.

Of course, the obvious question is how the individual entity and their supposed bondage come into being? The individuated consciousness, limited by the physical confines of the body, finds no other obvious support in manifestation. It assumes and thus deludes itself into an identification with a particular body. This delusion creates a pseudo-entity assigning itself to the body-mind and mistaking itself as the doer of actions rather than seeing that consciousness lives itself through such body-minds. Ultimately, the body-mind of a human is a "throw away" of consciousness itself who is simply revealing itself to itself in a cosmic performance. We are simply the tin soldiers in a playful game.

Many on the spiritual path in the west have taken up

the belief in reincarnation and karma. Karma is simply the notion of causality, which clearly is in play, mistakenly applied to individual stories as though they were real. But stop a moment and replay how life really works. Causality is not and will never be confined to the individuals as we define them in our intellectual playground. The murderer may be the right guy, or he may not. Things happen without regard to individuality. Causality simply pays no attention to us. If it did, we could declare that life is fair. But we all know that we claim it isn't, why? Because consciousness pays no attention to our moaning and groaning that life should be fair. We are but a concept or story that we hold is in play "as if" it were the case. This is our bondage. Further, what about reincarnation? Simple. How could a concept, a mistaken identity created when consciousness hallucinates and responds as though it were real, be something of substance that survives through death. It is our silliness of arrogant importance, self-assigned or inherited, that has us think we are important enough to be so superior as to endure through the absolute itself. As Buddha said, "Events happen, deeds are done, but there is no individual doer thereof. There is no transmigration of individuated souls." Yet, humans, in their fear of becoming non-existent, create a story that has them living forever, but as an individual entity. When awakening occurs, it is evident that one never was an entity and never could be one. And no story is needed to realize that we have always been and always will be. We just do not get to bend consciousness to our beck and call and have us survive as the pseudo-selves we have conjured ourselves to be.

Now, it may be good to settle for a minute on how it is that our pseudo-entity comes into play. What we are, absolutely or noumenally, is unicity-absolute-subjectivity without the slightest touch of objectivity. The only way that this "what we are" can manifest itself is through a process of extension called duality. This begins with a stirring of consciousness called the sense of "I Am". You and I commonly call this presence. Because duality includes the very activity of dividing the whole into parts such that perception can happen, there become subjects and objects and now one can perceive the other. Thus, conceptualization usurps the underlying unity by assuming that cognizing by different entities is not done by one consciousness but that each identifiable object is an independent cognizer in and of itself. And the story world is created, which is nothing more than a fiction within which we all live. Noumenon is what we are, and phenomena is what we appear to be as separate objects in consciousness. Awakening is nothing more than the disidentification from our phenomenal self as autonomous doers efforting ourselves through a life of objectification and having our identification fall back to its original self, the noumenal you. That "you" is the impersonal consciousness that we all are.

One can immediately see that we simply do not have volition and that the notion of "living our lives" is a joke. Our lives are lived through our body-minds by consciousness itself. But wait. Don't we see, hear, taste, smell and touch within this extension of duality. We sure do. This is all a function of cognition. The body-mind comes equipped within its intellectual equipment to experience phenomena and convert it into story. But here is the rub. Whose story? There ultimately isn't a "you" taking delivery of such phenomena but rather "you" are simply the conduit through which such phenomena are happening. So how does one live? One simply, in relaxation, sees that living is happening. Once you see that you are but a character in a play, it is easy to simply let consciousness play you as your role.

I believe it is easy to see that the seekers question of, "What should I do to experience this disidentification?", cannot but be an error. There is no individual doing that is really happening. How could I prescribe a volitional activity, that is illusory, as the antidote to mistaken identification? I cannot. When the mistaken "me" disappears then the real "you" is immediately uncovered. It is a true coming home as it is your true birthright and often is referred to as "coming home".

At this point, you must begin to see that the pretension that I am talking to you or that you are asking me questions is but a ruse. The reality is that consciousness is speaking to consciousness itself. A pointer is simply the unraveling or the dissolution of the ego concept with the hope that consciousness will in that moment see itself for what it is. We already know, deep in our intuition, what is happening. We just need a jolt out of our self-illusion.

pointers to awakening

Let's summarize briefly what we have distilled here.

1. Manifestation and existence within manifestation are phenomenal. Phenomena is simply an appearance which is cognizable sensorially and is time and space bound. It is a vision, dream, story, hallucination and ultimately not our true identity. Unmanifested existence is absolute, intemporal, spaceless, timeless, not aware of itself, not cognizable or available to the senses, eternal and our true selves. Who says this? Consciousness itself. This is awakening. And until then consciousness attempts to cognize itself and cannot succeed because cognizing (there ultimately is no cognizer) cannot cognize that which itself is cognizing. That is a fancy way to say that the eye cannot see itself although it sees all else. In essence, the seeker is the sought. It is difficult to absorb this sense of things but it is critical and the all-important truth.

2. I, in my unmanifested condition, am the absolute absence of the known and knowable and the absolute presence of the unknown and unknowable. I, as such, am the totality of all phenomena and the totality of the known in the inconceivability of the unmanifested unknown.

3. Ultimately there can only be "I', the eternal I, which is totally unconditioned without the slightest fragrance of any attribute. There can only be pure subjectivity.

4. Phenomenally, what we assume we are ("me", "you", "him", "her") are only appearances in consciousness. In essence, we are stories located in our intellect and animated by consciousness and nothing more. How could one say that a story or appearance be in bondage? How could I, pure subjectivity, be in need of any kind of liberation? The only liberation from bondage is dissolving the idea of "one" that needs liberation.

5. Lastly, how does one know when they are making spiritual progress? The surest sign is the realization that there is no "one" that does anything. This immediately induces a lack of concern and alleviates any anxiety regarding liberation. The purpose of pointers to help dissolve illusion is the approach to induce relaxation. This ultimately leads to an instant apperception, the perceiving with no perceiver, that there is no autonomous entity.

Now all of this is the condensed, no story or pointer, version of awakening. It is not for everyone, but to many it is helpful to lay it out end to end. I hope this exercise has been helpful for you.

chapter twenty-four

———•◦ ⚬◉⚬ ◦•———

quotes from the universe

OFTEN, WE ARE BOMBARDED with quotes and comments from famous spiritual teachers and masters. I have picked out a few that seekers seem to both gravitate towards and ask about. If you want to have some fun, see if you can predict where I will go with the answer. I will nest each in a concept or pointer that we have treated in the writing thus far. Enjoy!

"I find that somehow, by shifting the focus of attention, I become the very thing I look at, and experience the kind of consciousness it has; I become the inner witness of the thing. I call this capacity of entering other focal points of consciousness, love; you may give it any name you like. Love says, "I am everything". Wisdom says, "I am nothing". Between the two, my life flows. Since at any point of time and space I can be both the subject and the object of experience, I express it by saying that I am both, and neither, and beyond both."

NISARGADATTA MAHARAJ

Here Nisargadatta is attempting to give the seeker the sense of what it is like to live in apperception. He is not the first and won't be the last. I remember reading Carlos Castaneda for the first time at about the age of 17. I loved his journey story. Carlos was born in Cajamarca, Peru and when his later books came out in the 70's I had lived in Peru and visited with the Shamans, so he was a favorite of mine. The Peruvian Shamans and Carlos constantly spoke of one thing. Moving the assemblage point of perception. It was not until my life in India that I understood what this could mean. Here it is again in the comment of Nisargadatta. Perception is commonly held as a functioning of the independent entity of "you" as humanity commonly holds it. Apperception is "perceiving with no perceiver" or the perception of pure awareness itself, which is who you really are. Notice how Nisargadatta weaves his experience of apperception into his comment. He ameliorates all boundaries that would have separate entities within his experience. His experience is not "his" at all as one might normally think it but the experience of all or nothing, wherein he plays all the parts. There are no subjects or objects, beginnings or endings, and everything and nothing are literally the same thing.

My Peru story has a fun ending as well on this score. You might wonder why Carlos and his Shaman Don Juan both spoke as though they could, as entities, move the assemblage point. It was a niggling, and I could not help but wonder. In 2006, after 30 plus years away from the Andean altiplano, I travelled there with my wife and children.

There on Lake Titicaca, to my amazement, I met one of the current "old" Shamans who I had known when I was but 20 years old. I asked him about this notion that the "doing" of the acolyte could somehow move the point of assemblage. He laughed. He told me that in the tradition all was taught "as if" that was a possibility until the Shaman could see that the seeker was ready for the final teaching. The final teaching was that the assemblage point moved in relation to the dissolution of the "I" and the relaxation created by the understanding. It turns out that that knowledge is deemed esoteric and guarded until it is ready to be taught in that tradition. In the Advaita, or Non-Dual, tradition of India, there is no need to be esoteric as there are so many paths that the maturity of the seeker eventually brings them to the final teaching.

> *"What business have you with saving the world, when all the world needs is to be saved from you? Get out of the picture and see whether there is anything left to save."*
> —NISARGADATTA MAHARAJ

> *"How should we treat others? There are no others."*
> —RAMANA MAHARSHI

Here we have two wonderful quotes that must be treated together. In my lifetime, the activity of "Saving the World" has become one of the central notions of spirituality. Spiritual folks are out there saving the whales, the climate, poor people, rich people, people with addiction and the planet itself. Wow, we must be pretty pathetic to need all of that help! Perhaps the biggest obstacle to spiritual development is the move outward to engage in world saving. "Why is that?", you might ask? Once the "as if" story of an ego entity is activated it, for all intents and purposes, freezes the inner journey. There is a goal that needs to be accomplished in the world of duality and an actor, the former seeker, jumps into the gap to play the role of world saver. Note that both of these masters speak from the same vantage point, that of no ego. Nisargadatta counsels to, "Get out of the picture". Who needs to get out of the picture? Why, the mistaken identity of "you". Isn't that the essence of all of the teaching? Why, yes, it is. Then see whether there is anything to save. See how? Apperceive. Remember that we all will simply play the perfect version of ourselves in manifestation upon awakening in terms of how our activity is cognized into ego story. If your perfect story is to save the world then that is what you will do.

Now notice Ramana's response. He skips pointing to the spiritual process and simply points out the obvious. "There are no others." We saw before how Nisargadatta played all the roles as there are no roles. Here is Ramana, in an economy of words, indicating exactly the same. You will likely understand this and then attempt to focus on your interior journey. That is exactly what you should do. But there will be an insistent interruption to jump in and save something or other. Just go back inside. We should not be surprised that after a lifetime of "saving the world" conditioning that our mind, like a dog with a bone, cannot help but return looking for the marrow.

"Between pure Awareness and Awareness reflected as conscious-ness there is a gap which the mind cannot cross. The reflection of the sun in a drop of dew is not the sun itself."
                                    —RAMESH BALSEKAR

Here Ramesh is pointing to the conflation of story, as I call it. The common assumption within all human searches is that intellect holds in some way the keys to outcomes. Our dogged belief in causation and the construction of the entirety of human thought around this notion creates a vortex that is difficult to escape. No matter how obvious it is that this might not be the case, the mind will come back to this assumptive thinking. We know that conscious-ness in action lives each apparent entity that we create in our mindscape. Yet knowing that does not seem to keep the mind from switching back to its causative and entity thinking. I point out in the basic understanding that the only way to a tangible understanding, not an intellectual one, is through intense and absorbed personal experience. This is the vehicle across the gap. Do you drive it? No, you do not. You can simply relax and let consciousness itself teach itself to the point of the dissolution of what you hold manifestation to be. There is a gap. Mind the gap. Again, you might find yourself returning to the conflation of sto-ry, an intellectual holding with awareness, an intuitional holding. In our life we have often engaged in story and feel how animated it is. This conflation is the one I utilize in *Story Theory* to backtrack to your authentic identity. But, in the end, it must be seen that the animation in the story is not the same as the story itself. A lifetime of holding them as the same ilk can be a challenge. But give yourself grace to have this new pointer take its place within you.

> *"Human beings, whatever they may think, do not live and exercise volition but are entirely lived. The importance of an individual life, and even the fact of living itself, has been vastly overestimated and exaggerated. Nature itself defies the human presumption of the "sacredness of life" with the strongest possible demonstration that life is purely incidental to the totality of the manifest, functional order."*
> —RAMESH BALSEKAR

This is a fun one! Here Ramesh is contrasting the two elements that form the movement in spiritual seeking. First, we have life as lived in our assumption as egos. That life, of course, would receive such notice and development intellectually that its very essence would become vastly overestimated and exaggerated. That is easy to confirm by simply taking a stroll through the machinations of mankind appearing in any media source available to you. In the old days we could have said, "Just take a stroll through your local library". All philosophies, science, social sciences, etc., etc. are based on the focus of individuals and their stories. Remember when we spoke of the cognition-story continuum? Humanity has chosen one filter generally to extrude all cognition through and generate stories that center around the ego. Here Ramesh accounts for that cognitive bias and then contrasts it against what is really happening in front of our eyes. We have a pandemic. Does it treat the famous and rich better than the regular folks? Nope. It seems to roll through human potential blithely ignoring their bios. How dare it? But wait. We have auto accidents. Do those account for the value of humanity? Not really. He who gets killed gets killed seemingly without respect to his status in heaven. How about natural disasters? Does the sacredness of human life matter to a climate event? Does not seem to. Even when people call out that God is enforcing his will one is left to wonder. When you see the hoops through which the pundits have to jump in order to twist events into God's personal will, one can't help but chuckle. What kind of God needs to go through all of that stuff when all powerful is his or her name? Manifestation gives you the perfect window to understand that we, as body-minds, are but a piece of all that is happening. Further, it is easy to see that such a happening is entirely unbothered by the destruction of humans as opposed to any other objects involved in the happenings themselves. A beautiful pointer to see how our confirmation bias generates our worship of ourselves as humans as though that were an exalted position. What would happen if that bias were dropped? Now there is a thought!

> *"Your expectation of something unique and dramatic, of some wonderful explosion, is merely hindering and delaying your self-re-alization. You are not to expect an explosion, for the explosion has already happened – at the moment you were born, when you realized yourself as being-knowing-feeling. There is only one mistake*

you are making. You take the inner for the outer and the outer for the inner. What is in you, you take to be outside you and what is outside you take to be in you. The mind and feelings are external, but you take them to be internal. You believe the world to be objective, while it is entirely a projection of your psyche. That is the basic confusion, and no new explosion will set it right. You have to think yourself out of it. There is no other way."

NISARGADATTA MAHARAJ

This is an amazing expression of Nisargadatta. It builds on the previous comment from Ramesh. We all know that the spiritual world is full of folks looking for an explosion of something. Many want to build a spiritual Disneyland as I mentioned earlier. Only in an ego world of machine gun like confirmation bias would the arrogance of humans show up waiting for some big explosion of spiritual awakening. I have some bad news here. It already happened when you were born. The only problem is that you had no developed intellect at the time to note the event. There was not even an established "you" that held that it was separate from your mother's breast. Damn, I guess we all missed that one! So, what did we do instead? We built a world that is exactly backwards from what the case is. We declared that the outside was the inside and vice versa. Then we sat down with our beer in hand and waited for the ground to shake from the explosion we all agreed must happen. So, here is the good news. You have already been awakened and will recognize that place the minute your perception shifts back to that frame. But it is not an explosion. In fact, pure unity is a quiet happening and while sublime, it does not compete with the mind candy found in the ubiquitous action flick. But wait, wasn't the journey enjoined because we intuitively felt something was wrong? Remember those times when you had a rock in your shoe and that was all you could think about? Then the rock was taken out and within seconds the intense focus around that "something's wrong here" situation was completely erased? There was no explosion when the rock was removed. Just a moment of knowing that all was right with the world again. Then you went back to focusing on yourself. Do not delude yourself into thinking you are so special that some Archangel is waiting to come see you when your moment arrives. That ain't gonna happen! And you waiting for it will not get you any closer.

"My Guru ordered me to attend to the sense 'I am' and to give attention to nothing else. I just obeyed. I did not follow any particular course of breathing, or meditation, or study of scriptures. Whatever happened, I would turn away my attention from it and remain with the sense 'I am', it may look too simple, even crude. My only reason for doing it was that my Guru told me so. Yet it worked! Obedience is a powerful solvent of all desires and fears."
NISARGADATTA MAHARAJ

This is one of the most celebrated quotes from Nisargadatta. Many times, he speaks of earnestness. You and I would likely use the notion of tenacity for that sense. The main thrust here is that the approach to awakening is one of total embrace. In fact, it is the total embrace of something very simple. The sense of presence, or the "I

Am" as Nisargadatta calls it. Nisargadatta heard his guru say that one thing was necessary. He took him at his word and funneled all of his focus and attention in the service of this one thing. One of the things to understand about the words of Nisargadatta is that he did not speak English. All of his Satsang's were in Marathi, his mother tongue, and all of what we read has been translated. You will note the term "obedient" that the translator has chosen here. I can tell you that one thing Nisargadatta was not, and that was obedient! I would say a much better way to express this is that Nisargadatta heard a pointer, and it promised an outcome based on his adherence. And adhere he did. Ultimately, as you know, there is no individual to obey and no individual to demand such. But consciousness living itself through you turns on the activity of adherence within your body-mind and that is what will happen. Yes, you likely come with some attribute installed in your software which responds perfectly to the Guru or a random billboard. But respond you will, no matter if you create a personalized story of obedience to illustrate that response. Remember this one as a guide to all pointers. No matter how intellectually convoluted the verbiage becomes, in the end it is simple. You like to engage in intellectual vaguery? Cool, so do I. But see that this is just a preference. The central movement in the journey needs none of that.

"To consider that the world has no meaning or purpose is merely to say that the world is not centered on humanity. Without his ideals and motivations, an individual is frightened of being a

*nothing in the nothingness of a purposeless world. In actuality,
man's ideals of "purpose" as the basis of life and nature are
nothing but his own conditioned concepts. Nature cannot be seen
in terms of human thought, logic or language. What appears
cruel and unjust in nature seems so only when the matter is considered from viewpoint of a separated and estranged individual
human. But the rest of nature is totally unconcerned because the
rest of nature is not human-hearted."*

RAMESH BALSEKAR

Again, we return to the world of the "human is sacred" concentrism. What is important and noteworthy
here is to see how the notion of meaning making is treated. In most any treatment of human development you
will be taught, likely with no examination, that meaning
making is the main step of human development. It is
the celebrated attribute of being human. But think for a
moment of all that we have covered in our little journey
together. Here is what we have discovered. Intellect is a
device of human contrast equipping us to differentiate
between objects in manifestation. What is differentiation?
It is another word for separation. Unfortunately, we have
taken this so far that we have memorialized such separation to the point of absurdity. So much so that we declare
the world we live within is composed entirely of separated objects. This memorialization is set in quick concrete by connoting each and every object possible with
meaning. This must seem to the casual reader like an assault on meaning and separation. It is only that because
we live so out of balance, we simply do not recognize

any other type of human living. Meaning and separation are a wonderful thing such that we can navigate manifestation. It is a navigational tool installed in our programmed body-mind. That makes it a wonderful thing as a navigator is a needed element in objective life. However, somewhere along the line we decided to worship navigation to such a degree that we moved our co-pilot into the driver's seat. This only happened in our mind, however, and we followed through with creating meaning to back it up. That meaning making crystallized into our confirmation bias which feeds one story into our intellect. Which story? The one of our ego-story being an autonomous author of our now mental journey. Notice here how Ramesh points out that manifestation pays no attention to our mental midgetry. The driver of all is consciousness and our rendering of a different driver makes no difference to the actual driver himself. It is as though the cop pulled us over and we switched drivers pretending he didn't see. He saw. Again, as a seeker, all you really need to do is watch. You will see that life is happening without regard to our meager stories to the contrary. So how is it happening? Now you are on the awakening journey.

"Reincarnation implies a reincarnating self. There is no such thing. The bundle of memories and hopes, called the "I", imagines itself existing everlastingly and creates time to accommodate its false eternity. To be, I need no past or future. All experience is born of imagination; I do not imagine, so no birth or death happens to me. Only those who think themselves born can think

*themselves re-born. All exists in awareness, and awareness neither
dies nor is re-born. It is the changeless reality itself."*

NISARGADATTA MAHARAJ

This lovely Nisargadatta comment dispenses with the spiritual nonsense of reincarnation. To be fair, reincarnation is no different than the more western notion of an afterlife. Both pretend that you are an assumptive, autonomous individual you likely think you are. Both the reincarnation and afterlife story extensions are the novel like fiction extended into a future that is mental in its' entirety. The dragons and fairies you invited into your blanket tent in your bedroom as a child are as real as the story of your extended life. Both are fairy tales. Why is that? You, as a sense of presence, are only "here and now". The rest is held in your story archive of your intellect. There is no real happening in that archive no matter your demands that there is. Birth and death cannot happen to you as a presence. Yes, you can write them into your novel of "me". But as we have covered, this novel is the detour out of presence. See yourself as the eternal pure awareness and consciousness itself as a happening will come clearly into focus. How will it look? It will look like the statements in this comment. There is no past or future and no birth or death can happen. You always are and will be. Nothing to be born or reborn here. Changeless reality cannot be storied as all story is a revealing of change itself. And if you see the opportunity here, take advantage of it. You will sigh in relief as you unload yet another burden of your thinking life.

"What the mystic sees is really very simple to understand, but it needs a special kind of intelligence and a special perspective—not an intensified intellect but a kind of transmuted intellect, which can offer a totally different perspective by transferring to a standpoint beyond itself. For the egoic being, the outer world is seen as the face of an enemy. The disruptive dualism from which all conflict arises is not in the outer world but with the false perception of the pseudo-entity who fails to see the world as his own reflection."

RAMESH BALSEKAR

What a wonderful quote. You must be feeling some déjà vu here. Here Ramesh combines two elements we have covered already into the perception of a mystic. Like moving the assemblage point a la Castaneda's Don Juan, Ramesh speaks of the transfer of perception to a point beyond oneself. And he again points out that there is a gap that the intellect simply cannot cross. What happens when awareness crosses this gap of intuition? The intellect learns and renders itself into a transmuted state conforming with the apperception it experiences. Much of the human pursuance of awakening is the education of the ego-mind to its natural co-pilot position. Once there it can be easily seen that all of what arises in the outer world of duality from a story or conceptual vantage point is simply the frame of duality which most do not even realize is there. That frame, of autonomy, is seen largely as and conflated with cognition itself. The mystic sees that frame and experiences the frame being discarded by consciousness itself to see itself in the proper perceptive position. When I say that the purpose of consciousness is to reveal itself to itself, this is the ultimate revealing. In apperception "you" have left the building but there you still remain as pure awareness witnessing the revealing.

> *"There is only one state. When corrupted and tainted by self-identification, it is known as an individual. When merely tinted by the sense of presence, of animated consciousness, it is the impersonal witnessing. When it remains in its pristine purity, untainted and untinted in primal repose, it is the Absolute."*
>
> RAMESH BALSEKAR

Remember the metaphor of the spider spinning its web and pulling it back again? Here in this comment Ramesh dispenses with the web of manifestation and concentrates on you as the spider itself. Ultimately, you are pure awareness itself absent any web that might be created as manifestation. That state, when conflated with the story of you as an ego, is called the individual. This is the state of humanity in general. When presence is the only sense coloring the absolute there is impersonal witnessing happening. Why? There is still the frame of two parts involved. Presence, which is consciousness of the prime mover of the web that can be created, and the absolute itself. One is thought to be perceiving or witnessing the other. But remember what Ramana said? There is no other. This is the purity of awakening, pristine and pure, untinted or untainted, and within which there are no parts or pieces. Think about this a little further for a second. Why do we say the ineffable cannot be even spoken? Language is the conveyor belt of the intellect. The intellect loads the belt with packages of separation as that is its only activity. The absolute is the absence of all separation. And even in saying such I have converted the description of the absolute into a duality. That, my friends, is the ineffable.

> *"Nobody can say precisely what electricity is, nobody knows what Consciousness is. Both are conceptual terms in dualistic language to denote a basic 'energy' that enables appearances to appear and being to be. When the necessary contact is made, we know the result as 'light' and 'life'; when contact is broken the result is 'darkness' and 'death'. The point is that the Source of 'energy' remains intact, intangible and impersonal. What we are is Consciousness, the basic energy, the vital current and not the manifestations."*
>
> RAMESH BALSEKAR

Here again we travel into the land of things that cannot be intellectualized. First, the point that nobody knows what consciousness is, can be seen on display in the academic world daily. What amuses me on this front are the conversations within the so-called consciousness studies arena so popular today. These folks bandy about the term "consciousness" as though all agree on what that might be. Then consistently the conversation veers into the definition itself and all hell breaks out. It turns out that defining the very essence simply cannot be done. So, what do we know? Consciousness is necessary for something living to be living. Without it, in humanity, all we are left with is a dead body. This is what Ramesh means when he speaks of "energy" that allows appearances to appear and be in perception. Then he goes on to include "you" in that very category. You are consciousness and, in that sense, as non-definable as ineffability itself. Now, if you want to insist that all can be captured and defined intellectually you can always go back to the academics in consciousness studies. I am sure they will be arguing for as long as you live! One thing to note here. It can be confusing to see consciousness and awareness utilized often in the same way. Remember the spider and the web? Consciousness is often used to describe both. Other times pure awareness or source is the spider and consciousness is the web. One way to better understand this is to break consciousness into continuous components. Consciousness at rest is the same as pure awareness and consciousness in motion is the web of manifestation. Often, you will hear consciousness described as the principle of activity. This definition corresponds to the notion of consciousness in motion but not at rest.

"You need both clarity and earnestness for self-knowledge. You need maturity of heart and mind, which comes through earnest application in daily life of whatever little you have understood. There is no such thing as compromise in Yoga. If you want to sin, sin wholeheartedly and openly. Sins too have their lessons to teach the earnest sinner, as virtues - the earnest saint. It is the mixing up of the two that is so disastrous. Nothing can block you so effectively as compromise, for it shows lack of earnestness, without which nothing can be done."

NISARGADATTA MAHARAJ

What a perfect reflection to finish our tour through the quotes. Here Nisargadatta points out two things necessary to your seeking. The first is clarity. How do we arrive possibly at clarity? There is only one way. Perfect perception from the assemblage point moving away from the body-mind creating perfect seeing. This is clarity. And what does it take to propel this happening? Earnestness. Earnestness is the insistent tenacity of single focus. Perfect clarity and perception on the back of perfect non-egoic efforting amount to non-compromise. There is nothing mixed or diluted in this movement. In essence, do it all with total embrace. Sinning needs to happen? Great. Go for it totally. Remember the grit of life and the Zorba that balances the Buddha are of this noncompromising nature of you own pureness. It cannot be overstated that in the end awakening is an activity in simplicity. Whether or not the intellect is obfuscating the movement of consciousness, the simplicity of apperception remains. Pure perception and pure embrace are the only two simple components of awakening.

epilogue

EPILOGUE

————•◦ ⦂◎⦂ ◦•————

SATSANG & AWAKENING

THIS BOOK HAS been harvested from the lively and enriching Satsang experience. That experience is the call and response of questions and answers in a spiritual gathering. Satsang is the word that connotes a spiritual gathering or meeting in truth. It is a time-honored part of the oral tradition carried on by the sages and mystics of humanity since time immemorial. There is something in the role of responder that allows consciousness to simply speak its words through a sage. It is as if talking is happening to you and through you. Many of us who have had the good fortune to sit at the feet of an awakened master likely have been serenaded with questions and their answers for most of the journey. For many years now I have responded as a teacher to seekers' questions from traditional Satsang, both in gatherings and online, and to corporate boardrooms around the world. Awakening can only happen here and now. All questions can be bent with a response as a pointer to awakening.

My first major exposure to this format was in my days

in the ashram of Osho in Pune, India in 1990 and the years that followed. Every morning a recorded discourse of Osho would be played as many of us would sit in the garden and listen. Then, late in the day we would dress in our white robes and attend a live evening discourse. There would be hundreds and even thousands of fellow seekers sitting on the marble floor of Buddha Hall amidst the noises of India as questions had been selected and answers would follow. It is still easy to shut my eyes and hear the words of Osho in his distinctive voice wafting into my head.

As I moved through my journey, I would read books in the same Satsang format. Nisargadatta's *I Am That* was an explosive experience. But the most impactful book was one by Ramesh Balsekar entitled *Your Head in the Tiger's Mouth*. Eventually, Ramesh would become a mentor to me in my visits to Mumbai and a major catalyst in pushing me to write and speak.

Many traditions have a lineage through which folks point at to establish their authenticity. The string of sages with whom I would be categorized have no such practice and would see it as a foolish exercise. Osho, Ramana Maharshi, Papaji, Nisargadatta Maharaj and my beloved Ramesh all spoke simply, as I have. They are a part of an oral tradition that sits in response to the questions of dedicated seekers. Why do I mention them? I revere them all, as they were instrumental to answering the only question that matters to a seeker, "Who Am I?"

Since I have neatly delineated wisdom as emergent through the mystic or sage and knowledge as an intellectual construction available within any intellect, I thought it would be appropriate to include the story of awakening of this character called Alan. Yes, such a story does immediately reduce the actual happening into what we all call the world of duality. But story lives in duality and is the last stop before the eruption of apperception transcends such a view. The best one can offer is such a story as it is our only means of communicating any possibility, even one that lives outside the medium in which it is delivered. Here is that story as it appears in my first book, *Awakened Leadership*, 2012.

From the occasional to the permanent. This would be the next segment of my journey. Even though I had accumulated a large number of experiential placeholders for awakening, I found myself still engaged in "seeker's energy"—always looking, looking, looking for what still remained unknown. Sometimes a direct realization of truth unexpectedly blossomed out of a pointer. At other times, I simply held these pointers as conceptual understandings. My identity with a thing called Alan did slip out of place from time to time, but it still had some solidity.

It was in this phase of receding identification that I found myself some ten-plus years after beginning my personal search. The trek had taken me through shelves of books, dusty roads in India, and back to the high-rise conference rooms where I had gone from a pup to a big dog. I felt grateful that my experiences of expansion made it easier for me to live with less turbulence and more peace; but although my misery index did not register at its former seismic levels, I still felt an internal sense of bondage. The cover on the seeker's hole had opened to allow in occasional sunlight, and I was still pushing to find my way out. Eventually, I had the conclusion that this might be the situation in which I would always find myself. In this state of relaxation, one more event was yet to happen.

November 11, 1999. It is hard to forget a day numbered 11111999. I was driving up the freeway to Century City to attend a meeting with Jerry Skillet and some investors who might back our still-new 24/7 Digital, Inc. As luck would have it, a well-known actor in Hollywood was so enthused about our idea that he had asked his attorney to meet with us to review our plan. This attorney was housed on the fortieth floor of the skyscraper inside the Century City complex. If you know anything about that hulking tower of glass, you know that a conference with someone on the fortieth floor means that you have hit a home run.

So, there I was, weaving my way on a typical mindless drive on the infamous 405 Freeway. The stereo was on, and my attention moved back and forth toward whatever was drawing it along the way. The only unusual feature of the ride was that the traffic northbound was moving nicely. Then, in an instant, the world turned itself on its head. There was no longer an individual named Alan who stood independent within the world and apart from its functioning. In fact, the sense arose that the entire manifested world included this Alan—and all of what was in that world could be felt at one time. People always ask me what that felt like. It is like the sweet relief you would feel if you'd been walking for miles with a pebble in your shoe and suddenly it was removed. The heavy weight of identification had been lifted from me; I flew like a cargo-less plane that never knew he had any cargo to begin with. In a word, I was free.

All I had ever known was the efforting that I was continuously generating to take charge of and live each moment. Now I could clearly see that the moment itself was bigger than I was; my attempts to control it had been, and always would be, futile. A new thought occurred to me: I was no longer living the moment; rather, I was being lived into the moment. My hands still knew when to turn the steering wheel, my eyes could detect the most efficient means to maneuver from lane to lane, and my brain continued to register thousands of inputs and translate them into correct action. For all intents and purposes, you could say that Alan was driving his car. But the felt experience was that the part of my prior functioning that assumed it was performing these actions had completely disappeared. What took its place was the sense of an open field in which everything was happening on its own. Whatever was occurring had a profundity that was as light as a feather, and it was clear that it only could be arising from a much larger pool of awareness than my ego had formerly occupied.

A half hour later, I pulled into the cement bunker that we call a parking structure and took my ticket from the clock machine, like any other driver. After finding a spot and parking my car, I walked into the marble lobby of the skyscraper, greeted Jerry in the manner that we were both accustomed to, dutifully punched the "up" button for the elevator, watched as the door opened, stepped into the box, pressed the little square with the correct number, and arrived at our floor. My actions were like those of any other person on their way to a meeting. Jerry and I then entered the conference room with its long wooden table, typical high-backed chairs, and ubiquitous water pitcher surrounded by crystal glasses, and we proceeded to negotiate an investment on the order of several million dollars.

All of me was present except for the part that believed it needed to conduct my affairs. There was no efforting and no sense of needing to push an agenda with some other, separate selves on the opposite side of the table. When the meeting was over, I said my good-byes, reversed my course, and navigated home, where I was greeted as usual by my wife. There must have been a cockeyed smile on my face because she immediately knew that something was different. In words that I am sure made no sense to her, I tried to describe the shift that had just occurred. Eventually, I realized that underneath her genuine curiosity and reasonable questions was a concern that she might not know how to relate to this husband of hers, who was conspicuously not the same man who had walked out the door that morning. I definitely had compassion for her predicament. I chuckled, the kind we always share when she needs to know it will all be okay. "Babe," I said, "it can't be any tougher than it's been up till now!" We both laughed and then went into the kitchen to cook dinner.

My good wife had done me the favor of opening the door to the understanding that I will always appear to others as they construct me to be. In the world of ego and linguistics, all I can share are pointers toward a felt experience that can never be fully communicated. As the weeks and months passed, I watched with great interest, and no little amusement, as not only my wife but also everyone else in my world tried to recalibrate their definitions and perceptions of me as an ego. This thing that we call ego was only a small piece of the whole that I now knew myself to be. It was no longer possible to identify myself with the former, limited definition of Alan, which I now understood to be merely the steppingstone to who I really am. To its great relief, the ego no longer had to strain under the weight of trying to hold together the functioning of my world.

Now, you can imagine that taking a warrior personality, melting it into the entirety of what is, and removing the illusion of doership might create some mental confusion. Luckily, it was easily seen that this mental confusion was also simply part of what was arising. The ego, which had located itself in space and time within my body so many years before, was now revealed as being merely a concept that allows functioning to occur within reality as we normally identify it. Since that time, whatever is occurring is no longer happening to me. Instead, the concept "Alan" continuously arises within "all that is"—and the experience of that arising has no location, for it is not within space and time.

It would be normal to ask at this point what the difference was between this awakening event and all of the moments along the way that only had the flavor of awakened consciousness. The answer is that all of those prior events had a beginning and an end. Due to their temporary, transitory nature, Ramesh designated these as "free samples". (He had once joked that the term was his marketing contribution to the world of spirituality.) And what did these endings consist of? Each time, the mind would once again reestablish itself, and I would return to being a separate ego within all that surrounded it. Another way to say the same thing is that the sense of being a subject in a subject/object world disappeared for a while—for me, that meant anywhere from two minutes to two weeks—but this disappearance would end with the arising of the subject, the ego-defined self, once again.

I often say that the ego operates in exactly the same way as an addict does. From years of being conditioned, it develops a felt sense that attracts it to the dramas within which it plays the starring role. This is much like the experience of taking drugs. In the beginning, the ego gets a wonderful high. Of course, that begins to subside over time, so our conditioning drives the ego to keep coming back for more helpings of drama stew, hoping that it will keep being delivered, piled high and piping hot. And when the plate comes back empty, or close to empty, the ego— like all addicts—cannot help but go back one more time, still craving the fullest plate it can get. During the long period when the free samples were becoming more delicious and started to last longer, I kept returning to the addict's seat at the banquet table of turbulent drama. But at the moment of awakening, I realized that I would never need to pull up a chair to that table again.

How had I reached this point? The mind had, in essence, been fasting. That is to say, over time, the ego had been receiving fewer and fewer meals from the simmering pots of high drama. Without any conceptual wrangling, I simply arrived at the recognition that peace, as boring as it might seem to the ego, is the natural condition of human consciousness. With that realization, the high of being an ego on center stage no longer was irresistible. My identification had shifted to no place and no thing. The body-mind called Alan was still completely involved in the events around him, but there was nobody left who had the capacity to fixate on any particular aspect of these events. Thoughts still arose, as they always had and still do, but since there was no ego structure to support them, they would simply recede.

I now felt the rigid skin-boundaries of my old self sloughing off, with no new tough exterior to replace it. Over the years, I had been repeatedly told, "All there is, is consciousness." Now I understood this completely. I had become—in fact, I always had been—part of all that is happening, and all of it is happening within me. I could have said that I was in the flow, except that the flow and I were the same thing. No longer stuck in identification, I had become the container in which it all takes place.

From this perspective—and that term is not even accurate because it implies a fixed positionality that no longer held any meaning for me—the layer of chaos beneath the stability that the ego likes to pretend is there became more than my friend; it became me. Like a championship surfer who has become so skilled that she easily maintains perfect balance on continuously shifting waves, a seeker is no longer afraid of drowning in the surf of unpredictable experience that cannot be controlled. She has come to understand that the stuff of life is extracted from the chaos of manifestation. Instead of denying its presence, she enters into it. And in this relaxed communion with the unknown, she is aware that, once on her board, she can cut through the waves without thinking about how she does it, enjoying every effortless movement. What's more, she no longer has to chase that abstract ideal called the perfect wave. Every wave is perfect in its own way.

Lineage of a Sort

Ramana Maharshi

One of India's most famous saints in the early 1900's. Ramana was considered the modern-day Father of Non-Duality or Advaita. His notion of Self Inquiry into the sense of "I Am" is considered the cornerstone in the path of wisdom. Ramana created his ashram in Arunachala and gave Satsang daily until his death in 1950. That community is still in service and widely popular among seekers to this day.

Nisargadatta Maharaj

Nisargadatta is best known for his spiritual classic *I Am That*. The iconic yellow and black book can be seen from the streets of Mumbai to Santa Monica front rooms. Tangibility of the "I Am" or presence was his signature pointer. He was the predecessor to Ramesh Balsekar who took over his Satsang as he neared death in 1981. Nisargadatta taught on the 4th floor above his beedi (Indian cigarettes) shop in the red-light district of Mumbai happily puffing throughout his talks. He was famous for his short fuse. Ramesh would often tease me as being the American version of this hot-tempered sage.

Osho

A brilliant, awakened master and provocateur. His impish grin and philosophic insight were a rare combination. When hearing him discuss the ego, I knew he knew. This moment ignited my full-time search and years in India. He was previously known as Bhagwan Rajneesh and tagged as the Sex Guru with his collection of Rolls Royce's. He passed in 1990 leaving an ashram brimming over in activity until this day.

PAPAJI

Also known as Poonjaji, his real name was H.W.L. Poonja. Papaji held small Satsangs in his Indian village of Lucknow until his death in 1997. He was a direct and simple man with an omnipresent giggle. His awakening occurred while with Ramana Maharshi and he taught tirelessly the pointers of non-duality. He spawned many in the West, such as Prasad, that teach to this day.

RAMESH BALSEKAR

Ramesh, at his retirement at age 65, became a translator for foreign visitors to the Satsang of Nisargadatta Maharaj. A graduate of the London School of Economics and CEO of the Bank of India, Ramesh became the perfect mentor for me. Upon meeting him in Mumbai, where he gave Satsang daily, I became a daily visitor for long tea sessions in the afternoons. His guidance was instrumental in the creation of *Story Theory* and my pointers for the western audience. He passed in 2009.

ROBERT ADAMS

An American saint who saw a vision of Ramana Maharshi as a child and ultimately was his disciple. The story goes that his parents sent him to Paramahansa Yogananda, of

Self Realization Fellowship fame, in Southern California. While there he saw a picture of Ramana on the wall and immediately identified him as his visitor in vision as a child. Yogananda sent him forthwith to Ramana in Arunachala. He spent most of his years giving Satsang in Santa Monica and Sedona. His writings are silky smooth and full of pointers that softly beckon.

Prasad
An American from New York who spent his seeking time with Papaji after teaching for years in Harbin Hot Springs with an Osho therapist. Prasad began his Satsang in Encinitas in 1997 where I connected the wisdom of Osho to the Non-Dual approach of pointers. Prasad was particularly adept at deconstructing tangible story for the seeker. Prasad became a dear friend, and we have coffee whenever our paths cross to this day.

Milton Friedman
The University of Chicago economist won his Nobel prize in 1976. In 1977 I was assigned to be his helper in a large antitrust suit involving IBM, one of my Price Waterhouse clients at the time. The story is that he demanded a CPA that could "do sentences and paragraphs". As a well-known talker, folks humorously pointed in my direction and to their surprise he bit. He enjoyed the parry and thrust of sharp but constructive argumentation in economic theory. An idealistic 60's kid, such as me, fit the bill perfectly.

PETER DRUCKER

Peter is often referred to as "the father of modern management". In 1989, I enrolled in a graduate course of study in Philosophy at Claremont Graduate School. At the time, I was somewhat well known as a Merger/Acquisition resource and Peter was mystified that someone with my background would have enrolled in his management program at the same school. This led to our first meeting on his patio, which led to many more. I considered him a mentor. Peter was convinced that corporations would soon have to take the mantle of cultural and societal responsibility and that leadership would need to be expanded to include such. In me he found a spiritual seeker that was expanding those boundaries and he was a big supporter of my trek to India. Peter passed in 2005.

STEPHEN COVEY

Stephen Covey is best known as the author of *7 Habits of Highly Effective People*. I knew him as a professor of Organizational Development. My father was his student some 20 years earlier than I and he remembered me as a child. Some 10 years after graduation from BYU, Stephen engineered a seat for me on the Board of Directors in the School of Management at BYU which gave him access and time with me several weeks throughout a 3-year period from 1985 until 1988. It was his mentorship that thrust me into the "leadership as a spiritual path" notion that seems so apparent today. He, like Peter, as a big supporter of my journey to India. Stephen passed in 2012.

GRANDPA ED

I was lucky to be the oldest grandson of Edward Leitner. A prototypical Northern Californian dedicated to his grandson not becoming a "taco eater", a fate of many Southern Californians in his mind. Grandpa was my first mentor of what would become a string of grandfather mentors in my life. He taught me story, philosophy, and living the tangible life of a Zorba. I was lucky to have him until the age of 39 and I sat at his bedside with my childhood teddy bear in his last days. To the end we shared stories and laughter. His smirk was that of Osho, his intellect that of Ramesh, his heart that of Papaji, and his presence that of Ramana. I see him to this day everywhere I look.

CPSIA information can be obtained
at www.ICGtesting.com
Printed in the USA
BVHW071410211221
624592BV00002B/123